An Inspector Calls

J.B. Priestley

Guide written by
Stewart Martin

BPP Letts Educational Ltd

First published 1988
Reprinted 1993
by BPP (Letts Educational) Ltd
Aldine House, Aldine Place, London W12 8AW

Illustrations: Betty Eberl

© Stewart Martin and John Mahoney 1988, 1993

All our Rights Reserved. No part of this publication may be reproduced, stored in a retrieval system, or transmitted, in any form or by any means, electronic, mechanical, photocopying, recording or otherwise, without the prior permission of BPP (Letts Educational) Ltd

This series of literature guides has been conceived and developed by John Mahoney and Stewart Martin

---

Stewart Martin is an Honours graduate of Lancaster University, where he read English and Sociology. He has worked both in the UK and abroad as a writer, a teacher, and an educational consultant. He is married with three children, and is currently Deputy Headteacher at Ossett School in West Yorkshire.

John Mahoney has taught English for twenty years. He has been head of the English department in three schools and has wide experience of preparing students at all levels for most examination boards. He has worked both in the UK and North America producing educational books and computer software on English language and literature.

British Library Cataloguing in Publication Data
  Martin, Stewart
  An inspector calls: J. B. Priestley: guide.—
  (Guides to literature).
  1. Drama in English. Priestley, J. B.
  An inspector calls – Study outlines
  I. Title II. Priestley, J. B.
  (John Boynton), 1894–1984 III. Series
  822'.912

ISBN 1 85758 135 0

Printed and bound in Great Britain by
Staples Printers St Albans Limited at The Priory Press

Contents

	Page
To the student	4
J.B. Priestley	5
The setting of *An Inspector Calls*	11
Time-chart of *An Inspector Calls*	12
Understanding *An Inspector Calls* *(An exploration of the major topics and themes in the play)*	17
Analysis chart *(This shows important events, where they happen, time sequence, characters, and where to find them in the text and this guide.)*	20
Finding your way around the commentary	22
Commentary	25
Characters in the play	57
What happens in each act	65
Coursework and preparing for the examination	73
Studying the text	73
Writing the essay	74
Sitting the examination	76
Glossary of literary terms	78

To the student

This study companion to your English literature text acts as a guide to the novel or play being studied. It suggests ways in which you can explore content and context, and focuses your attention on those matters which will lead to an understanding of, and an appreciative and sensitive response to, the work of literature being studied.

Whilst this guide covers all those aspects dealt with in the traditional-style study aid, it is more importantly a flexible companion to study, enabling you to organize the patterns of study and priorities which reflect your particular needs at any given moment.

Whilst in many places descriptive, it is never prescriptive, always encouraging a sensitive personal response to a work of literature, rather than the shallow repetition of others' opinions. Such objectives have always been those of the good teacher, and will assist the student to gain high grades in GCSE examinations in English literature. These same factors are also relevant to students who are doing coursework in English literature for the purposes of continuous assessment.

The major part of this guide is the 'Commentary' where you will find a detailed commentary and analysis of all the important things you should know and study for your examination. There is also a section giving practical help on how to study a set text, write the type of essay that will gain high marks, prepare coursework and a guide to sitting examinations.

Used sensibly, this guide will be invaluable in your studies and help ensure your success in the course.

J.B. Priestley

John Boynton Priestley was born in Bradford in 1894. He attended Belle Vue Grammar School there, where his father Jonathan Priestley had once taught for some years, before becoming Head at another local school. Priestley's mother died soon after he was born, and he did not remember her at all. Priestley's home life was comfortable and generally happy. His father re-married, and his step-mother was kind, gentle and loving, as was his father.

Priestley left school at seventeen and worked for a living thereafter. His decision to leave school was based upon his desire to write; school held no further interest for him, and he felt the need to spend time gaining experience as a writer. He worked in the wool trade for a while, of which Bradford was an important centre. By his own accounts he was an appallingly bad worker: lazy, careless and a dreadful timekeeper. Later in life, he could not imagine how he had escaped being sacked.

His main concern at this time in his life was to get home to his room upstairs in the attic and write. His ambition was to own a cottage on the moors and earn a pound a week, which in those days would buy about two kilograms of good tobacco, twenty new hardback books or about a week's holiday. Priestley had no ambition to leave Bradford, which he loved and saw as having all that he needed. From 1913 his work began to be published, mostly in magazines and newspapers, some of it unpaid.

The coming of the First World War (1914–18) changed everything. Priestley joined the Army in September 1914 and became a member of the Duke of Wellington's Regiment. He could never explain why he joined up; he felt that he went 'at a signal from the unknown . . .'.

Priestley hated the war, remembering it as a time of pain and grief. It was during the war that he first encountered the English class system. Officers were appointed mainly because they were 'gentlemen'; Priestley found them incredibly stupid and complacent. He saw disasters happening every day, as the war became one continuous slaughter; this was largely due, he felt, to the insanity of the High Command. He found himself 'deeply divided between the tragedy and comedy of it'.

In 1916 Priestley was buried alive, injured and partly deafened during a mortar attack. He was sent back to England, eventually recovering and returning to the front in the summer of 1918. He was partly gassed during an attack soon after, and discharged from the Army, unfit for active service. Shortly after this the war ended.

After the war he was awarded an ex-officer's grant and successfully studied for a degree at Trinity Hall, Cambridge. He then turned down several offers of academic jobs, and settled in London. He gained a reputation as a serious critic with books like *The English Comic Characters* (1925) and *The English Novel* (1927), and as a novelist with his third and fourth books, *The Good Companions* (1929) and *Angel Pavement* (1930), which established him as an international success. He came to know H.G. Wells, George Bernard Shaw, Arnold Bennett and other famous writers. His first play, *Dangerous Corner,* was produced in 1932. It was successful at once and after this Priestley wrote regularly for the theatre.

Dangerous Corner and *An Inspector Calls*, although written many years apart, have in common a preoccupation with imagined shifts and swirls in time. In *Dangerous Corner* the ending of the play almost repeats the beginning – a dangerous corner in a conversation is turned, leading to catastrophe at the beginning, while at the end it is turned safely. In both plays Priestley contrasts a 'real' and an 'imagined' reality. *Dangerous Corner* and *An Inspector Calls* have two time-schemes, one of which is possible, and one of which is real, and we the audience have to decide which is which.

Priestley's most famous plays about time are *Time and the Conways* and *I Have Been Here Before* (both 1937). In the first play, all the characters move into the future by several years in the second act (a kind of flash-forward, as opposed to a flash-back) and are then brought back to the present in the third act. In Act Two, we see how the bright hopes of the Conways are not realized in the future, but in Act Three, they are still unaware of this. This makes much of what they say in Act Three about their hopes for the future very sad. In *I Have Been Here Before,* a professor intervenes in the lives of three people, whose lives he has seen wrecked. He wishes to persuade them to alter their behaviour to avoid disaster. In a similar way the Inspector of *An Inspector Calls* wishes to teach the other characters something about themselves which will prevent a recurrence of past disasters. Both plays use ideas related to premonition or reincarnation. The circular construction of *An Inspector Calls* also reinforces Priestley's message that there is no escape from responsibility for our own actions.

Priestley was much intrigued by the idea of time, and the writer who had perhaps the greatest influence upon him on this subject was J.W. Dunne. Many of the ideas which Dunne expressed were well known in Priestley's day, as was Dunne himself. His writings were a popular mixture of mathematics, technology and philosophy. In his then very popular book, *An Experiment With Time,* Dunne explains the notion of time as a fourth dimension through which we all travel, and he stresses the importance of dreams and their meanings in understanding the world as it 'really' is. Although much of Dunne's work was mathematical, his main ideas were expressed in general terms and were a major influence on Priestley and his times.

As far as Dunne's time-theory applies to *An Inspector Calls*, we see past, present and future entangled together with each other, as in a dream. At the end of the play we are uncertain whether what we have seen has been a flash-forward to what is yet to happen, or a flash-back to what has already happened. The boundaries between past, present and future have been blurred. What we think will happen after the *real* police inspector calls depends on what we think has just happened in front of us on stage or, to be more accurate, *when* we think these events have happened or will happen.

Other writers who also fascinated Priestley included E.A. Abbott, and the nowadays less well-known writer P.D. Ouspensky, who wrote *A New Model for the Universe.* Ouspensky's ideas feature in all of Priestley's 'time' plays. Although not always grouped with Priestley's major 'time' plays, *An Inspector Calls* is, amongst other things, about time and some of Ouspensky's ideas are particularly noticeable in it.

Ouspensky thought that time was in many ways 'circular'. The implication was that a person's life was relived many times over. Ouspensky thought that intelligent people could change this movement into an upwards 'spiral' and thereby attain a higher level of existence. People of lower intelligence (criminals, lunatics) would instead move downwards to lower levels. This meant that more intelligent people could, when moving on their higher levels, sometimes glimpse incidents from their former lower track of existence, through hindsight. Certain very special people, whom Ouspensky called 'chosen' people, knew all about this and could sometimes interfere in other people's lives to help them avoid disasters and mistakes as they loomed up again in the repeating cycle of that other person's existence.

As far as *An Inspector Calls* is concerned, we could say that the Inspector is one of these chosen people who is trying to help Gerald and the Birlings avoid repeating their mistakes. Not all of his attempts are successful, and we see that only Sheila, and to a lesser extent Eric, succeed in learning anything much. Alternatively, we could see the whole play as some kind of premonition or dream, which could be interpreted as a view from a higher level of reality. So this dream would represent a new kind of reality, a more meaningful kind.

Priestley was deeply fascinated by such ideas, as were many people of his time.

Characters in Priestley's plays are often seen not as helpless people, blown along by events, but as individuals who can, if they make the effort, take their destiny in their hands and change things. This is possibly something which Priestley drew from his wartime experiences, for by the time *An Inspector Calls* was written, Priestley had seen not one, but two world wars.

During the Second World War, Priestley was very moved by the efforts and tremendous suffering of millions of ordinary people. Many of these people had been poor or unemployed before the war started, and so may have had little obvious reason to thank their country for the way they had been treated. None the less, their sacrifices were willingly undertaken, and made a deep impression on Priestley. Priestley has sometimes been accused of being rather too much of a political preacher, but his defenders argue that he merely wished to make his audiences think. Students will have to make their own mind up about which view they take, with particular reference to *An Inspector Calls*.

The family depicted in *An Inspector Calls* are contented, and a little smug in their contentment. Their contentment is shattered, but the play is also a kind of judgement upon society: the unexpected has been shown to be first of all a nasty hoax, and then a frightening prophecy. The Inspector makes the otherwise rather pat and perhaps too coincidental events acceptable to us by the sheer force of his mystery. Like one of Ouspensky's chosen people, he seems at times to know too much to be an ordinary inspector. At other times, though, he uses interrogation and insinuation in a way that suggests he is indeed an inspector hounding a murderer. The Inspector seems to be a mixture of each character's conscience, moving in a dream-world which mixes past, present and future, as in one of Dunne's mathematical time-warps.

Priestley's interest in time is just a small part of the life of this amazingly prolific and versatile writer. He never produced a single, outstanding work which critics could point to as an out-and-out masterpiece, and because of this he is sometimes ranked as a lesser writer than other famous writers of his age such as George Bernard Shaw and H.G. Wells. Priestley himself thought that he had perhaps written 'too much', by which people have sometimes thought he meant that he should have saved his talents for fewer, greater, pieces of work. But Shakespeare, for instance, showed no sign of ever 'saving' himself in this way, and it seems a doubtful proposition that if Priestley had written less, his work would somehow have been the greater for it.

Priestley's writing was as varied as it was prolific. In 1938 he produced a farcical comedy, *When we are Married*, about three respectable couples who discover at their silver-wedding celebrations that they have never been married at all. During the 1930s, Priestley was a major figure in the West End theatres. When the Second World War came in 1939, he became famous as a broadcaster. Between June and October 1940 Priestley did a series of talks which followed the nine o'clock news on the radio. To many people, he seemed to be the true voice of Britain in those dark days after the retreat from Dunkirk. His talks were often about trivial things, rather than momentous events. They were about the simple things that ordinary people held dear, about the things which they stood to lose if the war were not won. Priestley's speeches to the nation at that time have been compared in effect with those of Winston Churchill: both seemed to speak for the nation, and both had a great effect on national morale. During this time Priestley also wrote novels and plays which reflected the war-torn times, but which also voiced hopes for a better future.

After the Second World War, Priestley served as a delegate at the United Nations, and later played a part in starting the Campaign for Nuclear Disarmament. In many ways, he was like George Bernard Shaw and H.G. Wells in his concern for the problems of society. In *An Inspector Calls*, Mr Birling mentions the latter two as the type of men who 'do all the talking', and who should be contradicted by the 'hard-headed' businessmen; but Priestley sided against Birling in the clearest possible way.

It was after the Second World War that *An Inspector Calls* was produced, shortly followed by other major works like *The Linden Tree*, one of his most admired plays. Later he produced experimental works such as *Dragon's Mouth* (written with his third wife, Jacquetta Hawkes), further plays, essays, literary criticisms, social history and novels. His output over his lifetime was immense, running to over forty dramas, some sixteen novels, eight collected editions of essays, collections of stories, travelogues, an opera libretto, ten books of criticism, several autobiographies, broadcast talks, political papers, a sociology book, parodies, light essays, descriptions and verse.

In his last autobiography, *Margin Released* (1962), Priestley recalled what he saw in Bradford of the rich mill owners and the poor workers, and of how the mill managers would refuse the girls an extra shilling a week, but could be found in distant pubs turning the prettiest and weakest of them into tarts. Priestley used these memories in *An Inspector Calls*. Priestley's views were influenced by those of his father, who was a socialist in what Priestley saw as the best, non party-political sense: 'the man socialists have in mind when they write about socialism', as he put it. Priestley was politically active throughout his life, campaigned for the Labour Party and even stood for Parliament once, but he was never a member of the Labour Party. He said it was misleading to call him a socialist, probably because he did not like the party-political associations the word suggested. He saw the tyranny of big business, typified on the personal level by the mill owners he saw in his youth, as neither better nor worse than the tyranny of communism. Priestley believed passionately that the freedom of the individual was paramount, and felt that our concern should be for the 'millions and millions and millions of Eva Smiths and John Smiths still left with us, with their lives, their hopes and fears, their suffering, and chance of happiness, all intertwined with our lives, with what we think and say and do'.

J.B. Priestley was awarded the Order of Merit in 1977, and died in August 1984, aged eighty-nine.

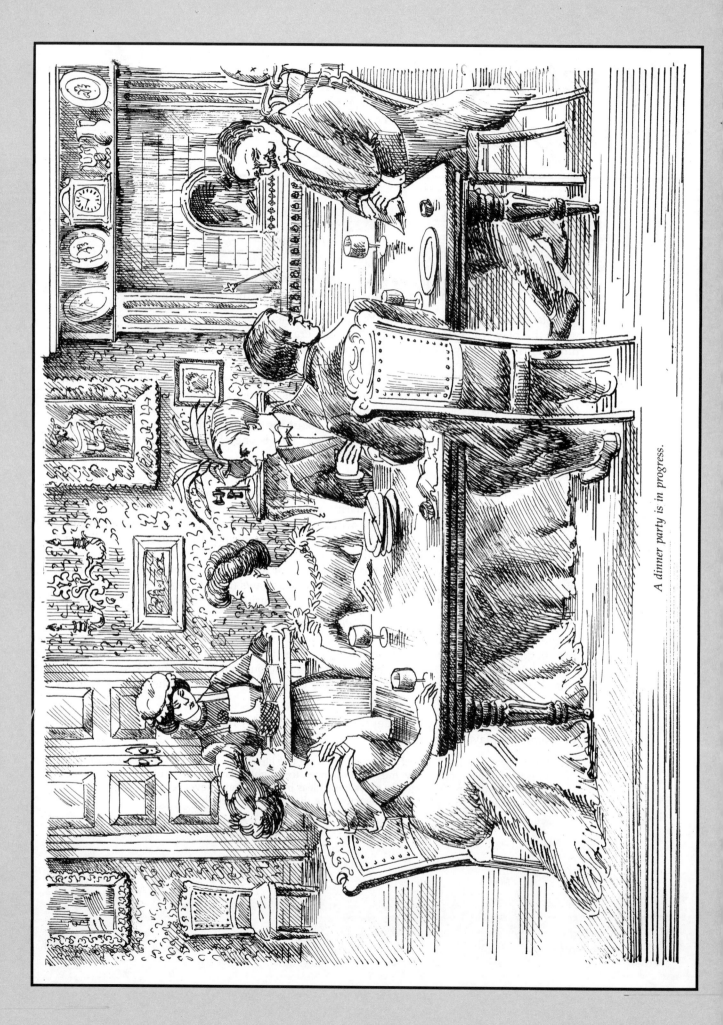

A dinner party is in progress.

The setting of An Inspector Calls

The three acts of the play all take place in the home of the Birling family, one evening in the spring of 1912, in Brumley, a fictitious industrial city in the North Midlands.

The play is set just before the First World War. Looking back on it now, or even from 1945 when the play was produced, the Edwardian era appears a rather comfortable and secure time in British history. Whether all the people who were alive then would have seen it this way is another matter, for not all of them were as well off as the Birlings, by any means. For people like the Birlings, times were good; but for the Eva Smiths of this world, it was different – they had little support from trade unions in those days, and there was not much in the way of legislation to save them from exploitation. The period makes a good setting for the play, because although a great deal about the society of the time seems attractive and comfortable, this is so only on the surface. This is one of the major points which the play makes about human relations in general.

Women were very much less well paid than men in those days, and unemployment meant real suffering. There was little in the way of state support for the destitute and unemployed, by today's standards: charity was very much the province of the Mrs Birlings of this world. The events of the play would seem much less believable if the setting had been more modern; and of course the chilling irony which rings through many of Birling's complacent predictions about the future would have been lost. Whilst Priestley was not trying to produce an advertisement for socialism, nor writing a party-political manifesto, he was none the less pointing out that there are serious flaws in any system which allows the disadvantaged Eva Smiths of this world to exist alongside the privileged Arthur Birlings.

As a final note about *An Inspector Calls*, it should be remembered that Priestley quite deliberately wrote a play, not a novel. Students should ensure that they go and see a production of the play, if this is at all possible; it is difficult to over-emphasize how important this is. There is a film version of the drama, but as it uses flashback techniques to reveal the life of Eva Smith, it is intrinsically different in 'feeling' to the play and, many feel, is much less effective.

Students would do well to consider carefully how Priestley himself stressed the importance of seeing his plays performed:

> My plays are meant to be *acted* not read. They are not literary . . . but at their best intensely and triumphantly theatrical. They moved audiences to laughter and tears, which is what should happen in the theatre. Though my plays have ideas in them, I have never regarded the theatre as a medium for ideas – the plays and the actors are there to move people . . .

Time-chart of An Inspector Calls

> When the war is won, it must be one of our aims to work to establish a state of society where the advantages and privileges which hitherto have been enjoyed by the few shall be more widely shared by the men and youth of the nation.
>
> *Winston Churchill speaking at his old school, Harrow, in 1941*

J.B. Priestley's *An Inspector Calls* was first produced in the summer of 1945, in Moscow, and in London in 1946. It is very much a play of its time, and really can only be fully understood if the student appreciates the contemporary situation, for this is crucial to what J.B. Priestley was saying.

The war with Germany ended in May 1945: Europe was in ruins, and two of the cities of Japan lay devastated by the atomic bombs which had fallen upon them. Priestley was writing at a time when the United Kingdom was emerging from six years of war. As the war moved from near-defeat to the approach of victory, people had become increasingly concerned with preparing for the times after the war. Throughout, there had been a determination that out of the horrors of war must come a society better than that of the 1930s, which had been haunted by unemployment and unhappiness. People were hoping for a more equal society.

During the war itself, most British people had been forced to think of themselves as a single community, in a way that had not happened before. In the past, wars had always happened overseas, in countries remote from home. Ordinary citizens found it hard to feel really 'involved' in these wars. But the Second World War had been different: there had been the blitz, and the evacuation of city children into the countryside. People were thrown together in a way which had not happened before and, as a result, started to learn about each other and care for each other at a personal level. Additionally, the war created a remarkable sense of unity in the British people, many of whom felt that they simply had to stand together if the Nazi threat was to be defeated.

Many of the younger men and women, who carried much of the burden of the day-to-day fighting of the war, were determined that after the war they would make the world a better place. These intentions had been voiced after the First World War, but little had come of them. There was a determination that this time it would be different.

There was a general election in Great Britain in July of 1945. Churchill and the Conservative Party were overwhelmingly defeated, and a Labour government was formed under Clement Attlee. The last general election had been in 1935, and many of the people voting had not done so before: young people who had just emerged from the experience of war. The election result reflected the determination of the British people to start new policies under new leaders, who were not connected with the problems of the 1930s. The new Labour Government was committed to economic and social reform, and their triumph at the election reflected the mood of the times.

Many people hoped that the younger generation would build a new world and avoid the mistakes which had led to the war; this is exactly the issue the play raises: to what extent Eva Smith's tragedy was a result of the society in which she lived, a society which gave honour and reward to men like Birling, a rich man who exploited the poor for his own gain and used them for his pleasure.

Students should familiarize themselves with the chronology below, to try to get more of a 'feel' for the situation in which the play is set. Remember, the play is set in 1912 and so audiences in 1945 and 1946 would have been able to look back with the benefit of hindsight. This would, of course, have exposed a lot of what Arthur Birling says about the future as nonsense.

The play was first performed in summer 1945 in Moscow, just as the war ended. Priestley was being honoured by Russia in being allowed a three-month visit at the time, and his books were well known there, where he was very highly regarded. *An Inspector Calls* was a great triumph, both in Russia and subsequently in the West, where it ran in many European capital cities.

Chronology of events 1912–46

1912 The *Titanic* sinks on maiden voyage – 1,513 lives lost
1914 Outbreak of First World War
1915 Britain blockades Germany
   Sinking of the *Lusitania*
1916 Sinn Fein rising in Ireland
   Battle of the Somme. British losses: 420,000
1917 Unrestricted submarine warfare begins
   Revolution in Russia
1918 Kaiser abdicates, armistice signed
1919 Alcock and Brown make first flight across the Atlantic
1920 First meeting of League of Nations
1922 Mussolini's Fascists make their 'march on Rome'
1924 First Labour government, under Ramsay MacDonald
1926 General Strike in Britain
1927 Lindbergh makes solo crossing of Atlantic by air
1928 Women in Britain gain the right to vote
1929 American slump and Wall Street crash
1931 Labour government resigns – coalition government formed under MacDonald
1933 Hitler appointed Chancellor in Germany
1934 Hitler becomes Dictator
1936 Edward VIII crowned: abdicates after 325 days
1937 Coalition government formed under Chamberlain
1939 Second World War begins
1940 National government formed under Churchill
   Hitler declares war of total annihilation against his enemies
   France conquered by Germany
   Battle of Britain
   London blitzed
1941 Germany attacks Russia
   Japanese attack on Pearl Harbor
1944 Allied invasion of Europe
1945 Hitler commits suicide
   Atomic bombs dropped on Japan
   End of Second World War
   An Inspector Calls produced in Moscow
1946 General Assembly of United Nations opens in New York
   An Inspector Calls produced in October, New Theatre, London

November 1911. Eric meets the girl and makes her pregnant

March 1912. Mrs Birling refuses to help the girl.

April 1912. She kills herself by drinking bleach

Name: Eva Smith. Latterly known as Daisy Renton, occasionally as Mrs Birling.

Age: Died in first week of April, 1912, aged twenty four.

Origin: Born somewhere outside Brumley in 1888. No surviving relatives.

Description: Average height. Very pretty. Big dark eyes. Soft brown hair. Reputedly lively, fresh, charming and warm hearted. Articulate, mature and intelligent. Prospects excellent until September 1910.

Death: Died in Brumley Infirmary in the first week of April, 1912. Suicide victim — died in great misery and agony. Insides burnt out by strong disinfectant. Approximately four and a half months pregnant at death.

Cause of Death: To be decided.

Understanding An Inspector Calls
An exploration of the major topics and themes in the play

Summaries of themes

Lies

Lies abound at every turn in *An Inspector Calls*. Characters tell lies to each other, they tell lies to the Inspector, they even tell lies to themselves. Indeed, we see how some characters tell the biggest lies to themselves. The lies in the play are not confined to simple misrepresentations of the truth, as when Mrs Birling at first denies ever having met the girl. Some characters are made to see that their whole life has been a lie up to that point, and that they will need to begin all over again in their relationships with other people and themselves. Other lies in the play concern the way people define things like respectability or truth. These kinds of lie are what we normally refer to as hypocrisy. Of all the characters in the play, only Edna, the maid (who speaks a mere twenty-two words), tells no lies.

Love

Several kinds of love are depicted and examined in the play: the husband-and-wife love of the Birlings; the (supposedly) romantic love of Gerald and Sheila; the filial love of parents for their children; the family love of brother and sister; and the Inspector's love of truth. Other attributes of love are shown, such as affection, gratitude, loyalty and sexual love. Priestley invites us to examine all these different expressions of human love and decide how sincere they are.

Power

The play concerns itself with the way people exercise power in society. We are shown, character by character, how power has been abused in different ways, and how there are different forms of power: industrial, financial, physical, emotional, sexual, parental, and so on. Each in its turn has been abused. This leads to some characters experiencing a sense of personal guilt, while others try desperately to shrug this off. The reasons why people abuse whatever power they have are also explored, and we see examples of envy, pride, lust, anger, idleness and greed. Indeed, most sins are represented in some form or other. The abuse of power is fuelled by a person's selfish desire to feel important, and by their own insecurity. Priestley's medicine for this disease is honesty, but we see how some characters do not take this willingly. For some it seems that it may have come too late.

Pride

More than anything else, the play demonstrates just how true it is that pride comes before a fall – especially the false pride of some of the characters. Pride is shown as being all too often rooted in shallow soil, with no substantial roots to support it. Characters are shown as being able to reach an honest relationship with themselves and each other only by abandoning their false pride. Some characters are so unwilling to do this that we are forced to conclude that their pride has become some kind of self-perpetuating fantasy, which actually has no foundation in truth whatsoever. Such characters, quite literally, have nothing to be proud of.

Remorse

Remorse, or a sense of deep regret, pity and guilt for some misdeed, is not an emotion which is expressed by every character in the play. Different characters react to their guilt differently, when it is revealed to them. Not all of them show remorse, or shame, and some of them are so hardened that they refuse to accept that remorse is called for at all. We see that there is a tendency for the younger people to be the ones most likely to show remorse. Priestley suggests that wrongdoing is rather like a disease, eating away at a person from inside. The acceptance of the truth of what they have done is the first important stage through which characters must pass, if they are to recover their humanity. Remorse is a prerequisite for healing to take place.

Responsibility

Priestley's main point is that people must learn to feel a sense of personal responsibility, not just for their own actions, but also for the way their actions affect others, whether they like it or not. The play actually goes further than this, though, by pointing out that we all have such responsibilities forced upon us: we do not have any choice about this, it is a duty which we cannot shirk. The Inspector is the character who voices these views most strongly, although he is joined by Sheila and, to a lesser degree, by Eric. In this sense these characters act as the communal conscience of the other characters. The opposite view is expressed by Arthur Birling, whose driving concern is his own self-interest.

Status

Status, or social position, social standing or prestige, is something which some characters in the play attach extreme importance to. For them, it is so precious that nothing must be allowed to damage it. It defines their value as human beings, and insulates them from the unpleasantnesses of reality. Birling's panic at the prospect of having Eric's actions, and his wife's, made public is rooted entirely in his terror of scandal. This would irretrievably damage his status, and that of his family. Other characters, like Eva Smith, appear to have no social status worth speaking of. In the eyes of some characters, this means that Eva has no value as a human being. The play invites us to question the false reality generated by things like status, and to consider replacing it with something altogether more healthy, if painful, like truth.

Analysis chart

Act	Act One												
Incident number	1	2	3	4	5	6	7	8	9	10	11	12	13
Important incidents / Issues raised	A dinner party is in progress	Gerald gives the ring to Sheila	The ladies retire to the next room	Birling hints at a knighthood	The doorbell rings	An Inspector has called	Mr Birling is shown a photograph.	We learn of Mr Birling and the girl	Sheila returns – she learns of the girl's death	Sheila is shown a photograph	Eric would like to go to bed	We learn of Sheila and the girl	We learn of 'Daisy Renton'
Themes — Lies	●	●	●	●	●	●	●	●	●	●	●	●	●
Love	●	●	●	●			●		●				
Power	●	●		●		●	●	●	●		●	●	●
Pride	●	●	●			●	●	●				●	
Remorse				●		●	●		●		●	●	
Responsibility	●	●		●			●	●	●	●	●	●	
Status	●	●	●			●	●	●					●
Characters — Arthur Birling	●	●	●	●	●	●	●	●	●	●		●	
Sybil Birling	●	●			●						●		
Sheila Birling	●	●	●		●				●		●	●	●
Eric Birling	●	●		●	●	●	●	●	●				
Gerald Croft	●	●	●	●	●	●	●	●	●	●			●
Inspector Goole		●		●	●	●	●	●	●	●	●	●	●
Page in commentary on which event first appears	25	26	28	28	29	29	29	30	32	33	33	34	35

	Act Two												Act Three											
	1	2	3	4	5	6	7	8	9	10	11	12	1	2	3	4	5	6	7	8	9	10	11	12
	The Inspector begins to question Gerald	Sheila sees something 'special' about the Inspector	Mrs Birling returns	Eric is exposed as a drunkard	We learn of Gerald and the girl	Sheila returns the ring to Gerald	Gerald goes for a walk	Mrs Birling is shown a photograph	We learn of Mrs Birling and the girl	We learn of the dead girl's pregnancy	Mrs Birling blames everything on the baby's father	Eric is exposed as the father	Eric comes in	We learn of Eric and the girl. Sheila and her mother go out.	Eric is exposed as a thief	Sheila and her mother return	The Inspector makes a speech – then leaves	Was he really an Inspector?	Gerald returns	There is no 'Inspector Goole'	Was there more than one girl?	There is no suicide victim in the Infirmary	Gerald offers Sheila the ring again	The telephone rings – an Inspector is to call
	•		•	•	•	•		•	•	•	•	•	•	•	•	•	•	•	•	•	•	•	•	•
	•		•		•				•	•				•		•	•				•		•	
		•	•		•			•				•		•	•	•	•	•				•		
				•	•				•			•							•	•	•			
	•		•		•	•			•	•						•	•				•	•		•
	•			•	•	•		•		•	•			•		•	•			•	•	•		
		•	•		•				•	•									•	•	•	•	•	
				•				•		•	•			•	•	•	•			•	•	•		
			•	•	•				•	•		•		•	•	•			•			•		
	•	•	•	•	•	•		•		•	•		•	•				•			•	•	•	•
	•		•	•								•	•	•	•	•	•					•		
	•			•	•	•	•				•	•	•						•	•	•		•	
	•	•	•	•				•	•	•		•	•				•	•	•	•		•	•	•
	36	37	37	38	39	41	41	42	42	43	44	45	46	47	48	48	49	51	51	52	53	55	55	55

Finding your way around the commentary

Each page of the commentary gives the following information:

1. A quotation from the start of each line on which a comment is made so that you can easily locate the right place in your text. (Remember to read around the exact reference to get the sense of the passage.)

2. A series of comments, explaining, interpreting, and drawing your attention to important incidents, characters and aspects of the text.

3. For each comment, headings to indicate the important characters, themes, and ideas dealt with in the comment.

4. For each heading, a note of the comment numbers in this guide where the previous or next comment dealing with that heading occurred.

Thus you can use this commentary section in a number of ways.

1. Turn to that part of the commentary dealing with the act you are perhaps revising for a class discussion or essay. Read through the comments in sequence, referring all the time to the text, which you should have open before you. The comments will direct your attention to all the important things of which you should take note.

2. Take a single character or topic from the list opposite. Note the comment number next to it. Turn to that comment in this guide, where you will find the first of a number of comments on your chosen topic. Study it, and the appropriate part of your text to which it will direct you. Note the comment number in this guide where the next comment for your topic occurs and turn to it when you are ready. Thus, you can follow one topic right through your text. If you have an essay to write on a particular character or theme just follow the path through this guide and you will soon find everything you need to know!

3. A number of relevant relationships between characters and topics are listed opposite. To follow these relationships throughout your text, turn to the comment indicated. As the previous and next comment are printed at the side of each page in the commentary, it is a simple matter to flick through the pages to find the previous or next occurrence of the relationship in which you are interested.

For example, you may want to examine in depth the 'remorse' theme of the play. Turning to the single topic list, you will find that this theme first occurs in comment 14. On turning to comment 14, you will discover a zero (0) in the place of the previous reference (because this is the first time that it has occurred) and the number 15 for the next reference. You now turn to comment 15 and find that the previous comment number is 14 (from where you have just been looking) and that the next reference is to comment 18, and so on throughout the text.

You may also wish to trace the relationship between power and responsibility throughout the play. From the relationships list, you are directed to comment 6. This is the first time that both power and responsibility are discussed together. Here you will discover that two different comment numbers are given for the subjects under examination – numbers 12 and 11. This is because each character and idea is traced separately as well as together and you will have to trace them separately until you come to comment 12 – the next occasion on which both power and responsibility are discussed.

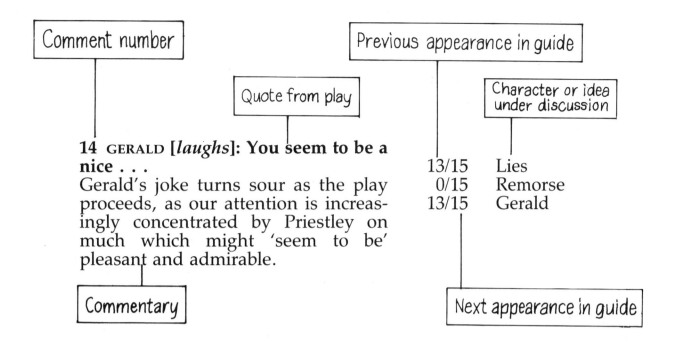

Single topics

	Comment no	Characters	Comment no
Lies	1	Arthur Birling	2
Love	1	Sybil Birling	4
Power	2	Sheila Birling	3
Pride	2	Eric Birling	4
Remorse	14	Gerald Croft	3
Responsibility	6	Inspector Goole	11
Status	2		

Relationships

Almost all of the characters exist in interesting relationships with the themes in the play. Below are some of the particularly interesting relationships which exist between themes and characters:

			Comment no
Lies	and	Love	1
	and	Remorse	14
	and	Responsibility	11
Power	and	Responsibility	6
Pride	and	Status	2
Arthur Birling	and	Sheila Birling	13
	and	The Inspector	11
Sybil Birling	and	Sheila Birling	4
Sheila Birling	and	The Inspector	17
Eric Birling	and	Gerald Croft	15

Commentary

Act 1

1 *The dining-room of a fairly large suburban house, . . .*
The entire play happens in this room, within the space of a few hours on one night during the first week of April in 1912. We learn that the room is 'substantial and heavily comfortable, but not cosy and homelike'. As the play proceeds, we see that this description is equally accurate when applied to most of the people we meet. The Birling household is materially well-off, but only superficially happy and united.

0/3	Lies
0/7	Love

2 BIRLING: **Giving us the port, Edna? . . .**
Mr Birling is at some pains to explain that the port is exactly the same as that which Gerald's father buys; he has even bought it from the same supplier. Birling sees Gerald's father, Sir George Croft, as his social superior, and this business with the port is a fairly blatant example of social climbing. Birling, we learn, is in fact very much a social climber of the worst kind. He wishes to increase his own sense of importance, but to do so mainly by going through the appropriate motions, rather than by actually doing more worthy things with his life. He may no longer be an alderman, or Lord Mayor, but he makes very sure that everyone knows that he once was. It is almost the first thing he and his wife point out to people, along with the fact that he is a local magistrate and a 'hard headed', successful, businessman.

0/6	Power
0/4	Pride
0/4	Status
0/5	Birling

3 SHEILA [*half serious, half playful*]: **Yes – except for . . .**
Sheila introduces the first of several incidents which jar against the happy atmosphere. These are the first hints of the unpleasantness which is to come, and show how disaster lurks just beneath the surface veneer of the Birlings' seemingly happy family life.

1/4	Lies
0/4	Sheila
0/7	Gerald

4 SHEILA: **You're squiffy.**
Sheila accuses her brother Eric of being somewhat drunk. Priestley achieves a considerable amount with this single reference. First, we are forewarned about something which will prove important – Eric's drunkenness, and his parent's ignorance of it. Secondly, we see from Mrs Birling's reaction that she has a very correct sense of propriety, and is rather snobbish. Thirdly, Eric's reply and Sheila's comment both suggest that there are things about them both which their parents do not know. Fourthly, Sheila and Eric both use slang expressions which contrast with the kind of language used by their parents – this helps to emphasize their youth and liveliness.

Each character in the play uses language, and talks, in a manner which helps to identify them and to reveal their personality. Contrast, for example, the pompous language of Birling with the clipped and incisive language of the Inspector, or the arch and stuffily condescending tone of Mrs Birling with Sheila's blunt and emotional manner. Such things not only affect the way we see each character, but how we receive what they say, how much weight we place upon it, and how far we allow ourselves to be convinced by what they say.

Finally, we see how Priestley has emphasized the natural setting of the play by using ordinary language and colloquial expressions contemporary with the times in which the play is set.

3/5	Lies
2/5	Pride
2/5	Status
0/10	Mrs Birling
3/6	Sheila
0/6	Eric

Act 1

Characters and ideas previous/next comment

5 BIRLING: No, we won't. It's one of . . .
Mr Birling is ignorant of historical and political realities. All he can see is that he is a successful businessman, alderman, friend to the Chief Constable, ex-Lord Mayor and past greeter of Royalty, who is about to climb out of the middle classes. He is about to have his daughter married into the nobility.

It quickly becomes clear that Mr Birling's happiness is also due to the prospect of Crofts Limited and Birling and Company one day working together, 'for lower costs and higher prices'. Birling seems to regard the marriage of his daughter as some kind of commercial arrangement, and throughout the play is inclined to see everything in such terms. This in itself is another of the play's ironies.

4/10	Lies
4/11	Pride
4/7	Status
2/10	Birling

6 ERIC [*rather noisily*]: All the best! She's . . .
Eric's comment is a hint of things to come, and is a clever touch by Priestley, because it arouses the audience's curiosity. It also fills in some background on character. Eric's concluding comment: '. . . but she's not bad really. Good old Sheila!' proves to be equally prophetic by the end of the play.

2/12	Power
0/11	Responsibility
4/7	Sheila
4/8	Eric

Gerald gives the ring to Sheila

7 GERALD [*smiling*]: Well, perhaps this will help . . .
Gerald produces the engagement ring. This is echoed at the end of the play when he offers it to Sheila again, although her reactions on the two occasions are very different. Notice how the ring is the one which Gerald wanted Sheila to have, not one which she may have wanted herself. The play abounds with such subtle touches, which fill in character and background. What do you think is being suggested here about the relationship between Gerald and Sheila?

1/8	Love
5/10	Status
6/8	Sheila
3/9	Gerald

8 ERIC: Steady the Buffs!
Eric uses an expression of the times to comment upon the way Sheila shows her pleasure at getting the engagement ring by kissing Gerald. Sheila is the most emotionally demonstrative character in the play. It is interesting that it should be Eric who remarks upon Sheila's behaviour here, because Eric himself has an explosive outburst of emotion at the end of the play. All the other characters are far more restrained.

The reference to 'the Buffs' is to certain regiments in the British Army, and harks back to the days of the Empire. It is the kind of command an officer might have issued to his men, to instruct them to stand firm and show no emotion or weakening. They were known as 'Buffs' because the fronts of their uniforms were at this time pale yellow. Eric is therefore asking for more self control. Whilst it seems likely that Eric's request is delivered with humour, it is interesting that Priestley chose to use such a term. By the end of the play it is clear that Mr and Mrs Birling, and Gerald, are emotionally stifled by their own self-control, whereas Eric almost loses all control of himself.

7/10	Love
7/13	Sheila
6/11	Eric

9 MRS BIRLING [*smiling*]: Well, it came just at . . .
The next time Gerald produces the ring will most certainly not be at the 'right' moment. Mrs Birling's admiration of Gerald's cleverness is echoed by her husband at the end of the play. Priestley has used many echoes and

7/13	Gerald

Gerald gives the ring to Sheila

Characters and ideas previous/next comment

parallels like this in the play's construction to bind together the drama in a very tight-knit way. You should be on the look-out for other examples of this, of which there are many.

---

10 BIRLING: Glad you mentioned it, Eric. . . .
Mr Birling explains at length his own uncomplicated idea of the world. His vision is rosily optimistic. He dismisses the prospects of war, strikes and all other problems in a very complacent way. The world is a very cosy place for Mr Birling.

Contrast is one of the main devices which Priestley uses throughout the play to generate tension. Here we see one half of a contrast, as we are given a picture of the Birling family as confident, happy, united, assured, prosperous, solid and self-righteous. Later in this act we see that much of this is completely unfounded, and this difference of mood makes a good dramatic contrast.

Priestley also uses contrast with regard to character and mood. Notice how each of the characters we are introduced to is made to contrast with at least one of the others. Even Mr and Mrs Birling, who we might think are most similar, have a clearly established distinction between them, and Mrs Birling behaves towards her husband just as the stage directions say she should, as his social superior.

5/11	Lies
8/13	Love
7/13	Status
5/11	Birling
4/17	Mrs Birling

---

11 BIRLING: Just let me finish, Eric. . . .
Mr Birling's wildly misplaced trust in technology is well illustrated by his reference to contemporary inventions and progress. But we soon see how Mr Birling's blinkered optimism about the future is no more 'unsinkable' than was the *Titanic*, which he mentions with such pride.

It would be too easy to laugh at Mr Birling, for we and the audiences of 1945 and 1946 have the benefit of hindsight. We know that his trust in the technology of 1912 is as sad as his assertion that there will never be another war. We have the proof of history that much of what Birling says is ridiculous. Birling's insistence on the importance of 'facts' is ironic in the extreme, for he is one of the last persons in the play to wish to confront the facts about anything.

But Priestley is not simply sneering at the stupidity of those people who thought like Birling. He is pointing to the way Birling's optimism is unthinking, unquestioning and blind. It is this refusal of the characters to think, to question, and to perceive the consequences of what they do which the Inspector comes to challenge.

Notice how the historical references made by Birling contribute to the play. Priestley uses them not only as a way to reveal character, but also as a way to set the background to the play's action. Priestley has set the scene, filled in some contemporary events, told us something about the age and its inventions and also given us a considerable insight into Birling's character. Yet none of this is done clumsily or in an obtrusive way. This very natural effect is difficult to achieve, but has been done with admirable skill by Priestley. You should be careful not to miss the subtle way in which background has been made an essential part of the drama.

10/13	Lies
5/12	Pride
6/12	Responsibility
10/12	Birling
8/15	Eric
0/16	The Inspector

---

12 BIRLING: Yes, my dear, I know –. . .
Mr Birling's reference to Bernard Shaw and H.G. Wells identifies for the

| 6/16 | Power |

Act 1

audience the views against which he is taking a stand. Shaw (1856–1950) and Wells (1866–1946) were both very famous writers who violently opposed everything for which Birling stands. They wrote pamphlets, essays, articles, plays and books in defence of the kind of ideas which so irritate Birling.

Characters and ideas previous/next comment	
11/13	Pride
11/15	Responsibility
11/13	Birling

The ladies retire to the next room

13 BIRLING: Thanks. [*Confidentially*] **By the way, there's something . . .**
Birling explains how he understands Lady Croft's alleged feelings concerning Sheila. Notice how this is something which Birling assumes to be the case, and that such concern should be 'only natural'. What does this reveal about Birling's views on what is 'natural' in human relationships?

11/14	Lies
10/15	Love
12/19	Pride
10/19	Status
12/15	Birling
8/17	Sheila
9/14	Gerald

Birling hints at a knighthood

14 GERALD [*laughs*]: **You seem to be a nice . . .**
Gerald's joke turns sour as the play proceeds, as our attention is increasingly concentrated by Priestley on much which might 'seem to be' pleasant and admirable.

13/15	Lies
0/15	Remorse
13/15	Gerald

15 ERIC [*eagerly*]: **Yes, I remember– . . .**
Eric starts to say something but suddenly catches himself, becomes confused and says nothing more. Mr Birling and Gerald are faintly amused by this, but the audience's curiosity is aroused: what special knowledge does Eric have of women and their clothes? Why does he suddenly refuse to go on?

Later, we realize that Eric's comment relates to his relationship with the girl. Notice how Mr Birling's rather patronizing comment about Eric contains an irony. The conversation between Birling and Gerald has been rather 'man-to-man'. Eric has been described as only a 'boy'. Birling remembers that when he was young, he and his friends were worked hard and kept short of cash, but 'we broke out and had a bit of fun sometimes'. This, together with Gerald's reply that he bets that they did, contains the suggestion that the 'fun' they had was with girls, and probably also involved their clothes.

Given the way we discover that Gerald has behaved with Eva, his innuendo seems to be quite in character. Birling, on the other hand, later adopts a typically hypocritical attitude to his son's dealings with women.

14/16	Lies
13/16	Love
14/18	Remorse
12/16	Responsibility
13/16	Birling
11/17	Eric
14/17	Gerald

16 BIRLING [*solemnly*]: **But this is the point. . . .**
Mr Birling expresses his philosophy that 'a man has to mind his own business and look after himself and his own'. We are to see how the events of the play make this attitude both dangerous and unworkable. It is no accident that this speech is followed immediately by the coming of one of those 'cranks' whom Birling has just been sneering at – as the Inspector calls.

15/17	Lies
15/23	Love
12/19	Power
15/20	Responsibility
15/17	Birling
11/17	The Inspector

The doorbell rings

17 BIRLING: Special occasion. And feeling contented, for once, ...
At this point the Inspector enters the action of the play. After this, nothing remains the same. This is a good point to consider what you have learned about the Birling household up to now, because the rest of this act will undermine most of what we have been given to see as the 'reality' of it so far.

[handwritten: What have you learned about the Birling household up to now?]

16/18	Lies
16/19	Birling
10/43	Mrs Birling
13/32	Sheila
15/18	Eric
15/19	Gerald
16/19	The Inspector

An inspector has called

18 ERIC [*Who is uneasy, sharply*]: Here, what ...
Eric does not share the joke between Mr Birling and Gerald. He attracts attention, and then suspicion, by his alarmed attitude at the news of the Inspector's visit. This clever touch by Priestley makes us alert to the possibility that Eric has been up to something.

17/20	Lies
15/22	Remorse
17/23	Eric

19 BIRLING [*after a pause, with a touch of impatience*]: ...
Birling is becoming impatient with the Inspector. Notice how Gerald and Birling are not frightened by the visit of the Inspector at first. They regard the police as their protectors, but their servants first. This is why, later on, both Mr and Mrs Birling take such sharp exception to the way the Inspector speaks to them.

16/20	Power
13/21	Pride
13/24	Status
17/22	Birling
17/20	Gerald
17/20	The Inspector

Birling is shown a photograph

20 GERALD [*showing annoyance*]: Any particular reason why I ...
Gerald is irritated that the Inspector refuses to let him see the photograph which he is showing to Mr Birling. The Inspector says that he likes to work this way: 'One person and one line of inquiry at a time'. Gerald is not altogether convinced, and the Inspector's tactic, which he repeats throughout the play, annoys people more than once.

The business with the photograph becomes very important at the end of the play, when Gerald realizes that by never allowing two people to see it at the same time, the Inspector may have been concealing from them the fact that several different photographs were involved. The Inspector's behaviour with the photograph is an example of Priestley's dramatic skill, and shows clever construction in the play.

18/21	Lies
19/22	Power
16/22	Responsibility
19/21	Gerald
19/24	The Inspector

21 GERALD: Look here, sir. Wouldn't you rather ...
Why does Gerald say this? Think carefully – is it good manners on his part? If it is, why exactly is this kind of behaviour 'good' manners? Or is it that Gerald thinks that there may be some scandal? If so, what could be his motive for not wishing to hear about it? He can't possibly think that it involves him, can he?

20/22	Lies
19/24	Pride
20/26	Gerald

22 BIRLING: Oh well – put like that, there's something ...
Mr Birling may well say that he thinks there is something in what the

21/23	Lies

Act 1

Inspector says, but he clearly does not believe it, because he continues by saying that he 'can't accept any responsibility' for the fate of the girl.

Priestley's main argument in the play is that people *must* accept responsibility for others, whether they like it or not. As Birling points out, this would make life 'very awkward' for some people.

20/25	Power
18/35	Remorse
20/23	Responsibility
19/23	Birling

23 ERIC: By Jove, yes. And as you . . .
Eric reminds his father of his advice that a man should 'mind his own business and look after himself and his own'. In the light of the Inspector's news about the girl's death, this reminder is embarrassing for Birling. It is also the first in a long line of embarrassments which he and other characters will have to suffer, as they come face to face with the truth.

22/29	Lies
16/34	Love
22/25	Responsibility
22/24	Birling
18/24	Eric

24 BIRLING [*surprised*]: Did you say 'Why?'?
Birling takes exception to the Inspector's tone, but his objections are swept aside as the line of questioning continues.

Generally speaking, the characters in the play seem to be so bound up with the Inspector's revelations about them that they do not notice the unusual way in which he talks. The Inspector does not just ask questions but, as here, makes comments about the behaviour and attitudes of others and passes judgements on them in a way which a real Inspector almost certainly would not. It is not until the end of the play, and after the Inspector has left, that the other characters seem to fully realize this.

Because of his general attitude, we quickly see that the Inspector is rather more than just a police officer investigating the background of a suicide victim. Here, for example, he goes on to agree with Eric that the girl could not simply have gone off and worked somewhere else, as Birling suggested. Birling's justification of his sacking of the girl is clearly not accepted by either Eric or the Inspector.

21/28	Pride
19/28	Status
23/25	Birling
23/25	Eric
20/25	The Inspector

We learn of Birling and the girl

25 BIRLING: Well, it's my duty . . .
Birling sees himself as a hard-headed, no-nonsense employer. His workers are paid the going rate for the job, no less and no more. He is determined to protect his own interests, and those of others like him. His attitude towards strikers is unsympathetic. Those he sees as trouble-makers are given the sack. He has no reservations about what he did to the girl, and is rather put out by the Inspector's attitude. Eric is faintly critical, but his father rounds on him forcefully and tells him to keep out of it.

Notice Birling's revealing use of the word 'duty'. A duty is normally thought of as something which people do for legal or moral reasons, something which binds them to their obligations. Clearly, Birling has no legal obligation to keep labour costs down; presumably then it is something to do with what Birling sees as his moral obligations. This tells us a lot about the kind of morals Birling has, and about how much value he places upon people.

22/26	Power
23/26	Responsibility
24/26	Birling
24/26	Eric
24/26	The Inspector

26 ERIC: He could. He could have kept her . . .
Eric consistently takes the opposite line to Gerald. Mr Birling clearly finds this increasingly irritating. Notice how Priestley has made the voice of conscience come, appropriately, from inside the family, not from the

25/34	Power
25/27	Responsibility
25/27	Birling

We learn of Birling and the girl

outsider, Gerald. Is there anybody else in the play who also acts as a kind of 'conscience' for the other characters?

Characters and ideas previous/next comment	
25/29	Eric
21/31	Gerald
25/27	The Inspector

---

27 INSPECTOR: They might. But after all it's better . . .
The Inspector points out that it is better for people to ask for the earth than to take it. The implication is that some people – like Birling – take everything and leave others with little or nothing. Understandably, Birling is offended at being accused of being some kind of thief.

Priestley wrote *An Inspector Calls* very quickly – within a week – and the play has about it a sense of breathless urgency. There is a very real sense in which the play and its Inspector plunge straight into the truth at the deep-end. This kind of approach can be found in many of Priestley's works.

The Inspector's relentless pursuit of the truth, and his frequent moral judgements, as here, almost smack of an Inquisition. He seems to want to torture each character with the truth of what they have done. Priestley's swift and sharp style is admirably suited to this approach.

26/30	Responsibility
26/28	Birling
26/29	The Inspector

---

28 BIRLING: Perhaps I ought to warn you . . .
Birling is proud of being 'somebody' in the local community. This is not the only time that he refers to his friendship with Chief Constable Roberts. Notice how Birling specifically mentions that the Chief Constable is a colonel – no opportunity is missed to try to gain more importance by name-dropping. The play's events illustrate the old adage that 'pride comes before a fall'.

What does all this tell you about the Birlings? Do you think that all the prominent people they mention would be as quick to name-drop about their friendship with the Birlings? What does this suggest about the Birlings?

24/35	Pride
24/31	Status
27/30	Birling

---

29 INSPECTOR: No, I've never wanted to play.
The Inspector's deliberate misunderstanding of what Eric meant provides a lighter moment. This is deliberate, for it helps provide a contrast to the serious revelations which are shortly to be unveiled. To what extent do you think the Inspector might have been mocking Eric's comment? Does the Inspector think that Eric's expression of sympathy is simply 'good manners' and therefore insincere?

23/32	Lies
26/30	Eric
27/32	The Inspector

---

30 BIRLING [*rather angrily*]: Unless you brighten your ideas, . . .
Birling says that it is about time that Eric 'learnt to face a few responsibilities'. This tellingly ironic remark illustrates clearly the gigantic hypocrisy of Birling. Just a few moments before this, Birling was denying to the Inspector that he could in any way accept responsibility for the girl's fate. Throughout the rest of the play, we see Birling's increasingly desperate attempts to avoid 'facing a few responsibilities'.

27/32	Responsibility
28/33	Birling
29/31	Eric

---

31 INSPECTOR [*rather slowly*]: No, she didn't exactly . . .
The Inspector points out that the girl did not *exactly* become a prostitute. In what ways can we see that she was, in effect, treated as such by Gerald and Eric, though?

28/48	Status
30/32	Eric
26/32	Gerald

Sheila returns – she learns of the girl's death

32 INSPECTOR [*slowly*]: **Are you sure you don't know?**
By making the Inspector say this, and then by having him look in turn at Gerald, Eric and Sheila, Priestley makes it clear that we ought to suspect that each of them does in fact know something. This device of guilt by implication increases the dramatic tension, and leads us to expect that more links in the Inspector's chain of events will soon be revealed.

29/33	Lies
30/33	Responsibility
17/34	Sheila
31/35	Eric
31/33	Gerald
29/33	The Inspector

---

33 BIRLING [*with marked change of tone*]: **Well, of course, . . .**
Birling changes his attitude when he is told that the Inspector has come to question people other than just himself. Why is this? Notice how it has just been pointed out by Gerald that it is what happened to the girl since she left Birling's works which is important.

32/35	Lies
32/35	Responsibility
30/34	Birling
32/39	Gerald
32/36	The Inspector

---

34 BIRLING [*cutting in*]: **Just a minute, Sheila. . . .**
Birling attempts to intervene. He wishes to settle matters himself, and does not want his daughter involved. We see several examples of this in the play. Who else behaves in this way, and likes to make decisions for other people?

23/52	Love
26/35	Power
33/37	Birling
32/35	Sheila

---

35 SHEILA [*to* BIRLING]: **I think it was a mean thing . . .**
Almost immediately after she has learned the background to Eva Smith's dismissal from Mr Birling's factory, Sheila is critical of her father. In this she is very consistent in the play, for in all three acts she tends to act as the 'conscience' of the Birling family. To some extent she is supported in this role by Eric, although he is a much weaker and more evasive character than she.

Why do you think that Priestley chose Sheila to fulfil this role? Consider how effective it would have been if the roles of Sheila and Eric had been reversed, with he as the 'conscience' and she as a 'squiffy' ne'er-do-well.

Clearly, our natural tendency to connect Sheila with Eva, and to see likenesses between them and their characters, has been deliberately encouraged by Priestley. This is clever, because it increases our sympathy for Eva by showing us the kind of happy life she might have had. Also, we are made to feel that Eva, whom we never see, is more 'real', because we can relate her to another character who is in front of us. This dramatic device adds considerable weight to Sheila's criticisms, because we feel that she is somehow speaking on behalf of the dead girl when she accuses the others of indifference, callousness, cruelty, pride and snobbery. The fact that the dead girl made none of these accusations when she was alive adds impact to the way Sheila makes them for her.

33/39	Lies
34/41	Power
28/44	Pride
22/42	Remorse
33/36	Responsibility
34/41	Sheila
32/55	Eric

---

36 INSPECTOR [*dryly*]: **I've had that notion myself . . .**
The Inspector's pronouncements are focused not just upon the Birlings. What he has to say applies to society as a whole. Priestley achieves the effect of making the Inspector's comments 'universal' by having him make the kind of statements he makes here: 'it would do us all a bit of good if sometimes we tried to put ourselves in the place of these young women . . .'. This broadens the theme of the play so that we can see that it

35/37	Responsibility
33/38	The Inspector

relates to all of us. The Inspector's comments often have this 'feel' to them, as though they were addressed as much to the audience as to the other characters on stage. This is sometimes true of the things which other characters say also, and you should be on the look out for examples of this kind of 'audience participation' in the play.

37 BIRLING: And then she got herself into trouble . . .
Notice Birling's choice of words. To what extent is it fair to say that on each occasion Eva Smith met up with one of the play's characters *she* got *herself* into trouble?

36/38	Responsibility
34/38	Birling

Sheila is shown a photograph

38 INSPECTOR [*steadily*]: That's more or less what . . .
The Inspector makes it clear that his purpose is to establish exactly who it is that has made 'a nasty mess' of Eva Smith's life. Compare this with Birling's attitude. Why exactly is Birling cross?

37/40	Responsibility
37/44	Birling
36/39	The Inspector

39 GERALD: I'd like to have a look . . .
Gerald asks to see the photograph. Interestingly, although the Inspector says that he may see it later – 'all in good time' – Gerald never actually does see it. Priestley is deliberately and skilfully teasing us. How different might the rest of the play have been if Gerald *had* seen the photograph here? This is one of the many questions which the play encourages us to ask, but refuses to answer.

35/43	Lies
33/48	Gerald
38/40	The Inspector

Eric would like to go to bed

40 INSPECTOR: Sometimes there isn't as much difference . . .
The Inspector returns to this key point throughout the play. It is his central 'message'; he wishes to point out to the characters, and through them to the audience, the real nature of people's responsibility for what they do and how it affects others. Priestley manipulates the 'whodunnit' formula to bring out the truth through the Inspector's searching inquisition.

The Inspector suggests that the line between guilt and innocence is narrower than people commonly assume. Sometimes it is very hard to establish which side of the line people are on.

38/42	Responsibility
39/41	The Inspector

41 SHEILA [*coming in, closing door*]: You knew it was me . . .
Sheila is the first to recognize that the Inspector seems to have some special way of knowing about people. Apart from Eric, all the other characters continue to see Inspector Goole as a police officer or, at the end of the play, as a hoaxer. Sheila is increasingly convinced that he is nothing of the kind, and that his strangeness cannot be explained except in other-worldly terms.

35/44	Power
35/42	Sheila
40/47	The Inspector

42 SHEILA [*miserably*]: So I'm really responsible?
Sheila is more ready than any of the other characters to admit her guilt and express regret for her actions. The Inspector makes sure that she does not get her part in the downfall of Eva Smith out of proportion, however, by going out of his way to emphasize that she was only partly to blame.

35/43	Remorse
40/44	Responsibility
41/43	Sheila

Act 1

43 SHEILA: Because I was in a furious temper.
Contrast this open and honest admission of Sheila's with that of her mother at the end of Act Two. The confessions of the male characters are similarly different – the younger they are, the more easily they are prepared to accept the consequences of their own actions.

Characters and ideas previous/next comment

39/46	Lies
42/46	Remorse
17/57	Mrs Birling
42/44	Sheila

We learn of Sheila and the girl

44 SHEILA: I'd gone in to try something on. . . .
Sheila describes the incident where she went to try on a dress. She had insisted on trying a particular dress on, even though her mother and the assistant, Miss Francis, had advised against it. In the event, she saw that they had been correct and that the dress simply did not suit her, and she 'looked silly in the thing'. It is clear that being shown to be in the wrong about the dress put Sheila in a bad mood. She subsequently took this out on the girl.

It is revealing to compare the different ways in which Eva Smith and Sheila Birling were treated. Eva's opinions caused her to be wrongly dismissed by Birling as a 'trouble-maker'. Sheila's actions were quite clearly those of a genuine trouble-maker, but she was immune from punishment for them. Instead, someone else was punished. On both occasions someone innocent was victimized because they were weak and unable to defend themselves. On both occasions someone innocent was made a victim of someone else's lack of human feeling.

41/45	Power
35/57	Pride
42/45	Responsibility
38/45	Birling
43/45	Sheila

45 INSPECTOR: And so you used the power you had, . . .
Sheila admits that she victimized the girl out of feelings of jealousy. Sheila abused her power in much the same way as her father did when he dismissed the girl from his factory. Between them, Sheila and her father contrived to ruin the girl financially. During the next two acts we are shown how the other characters in the drama ruined her spiritually, morally and physically.

44/48	Power
44/53	Responsibility
44/69	Birling
44/46	Sheila

46 SHEILA: Yes, but it didn't seem to be anything . . .
Sheila is the first to confess her guilt in the girl's fate. Notice how she at once repents what she did and makes only a minimal effort to excuse her behaviour. In this she is different to all the other characters, who one by one are increasingly obdurate.

Sheila is the character most closely identified with the dead girl. She is also the first, at the end of the play, to fight against the way her parents try to pretend that everything is normal again.

43/47	Lies
43/47	Remorse
45/48	Sheila

47 INSPECTOR [*sternly*]: That's what I asked myself tonight . . .
The Inspector performs the function of both questioner and story-teller in the play. He provides us with the framework of the girl's life story, fills in the background where appropriate and sometimes, as here, seems to speak for the audience; 'Well, we'll try to understand why it had to happen. And that's why I'm here, and why I'm not going until I know *all* that happened.'

46/48	Lies
46/51	Remorse
41/49	The Inspector

We learn of 'Daisy Renton'

48 INSPECTOR: Where is your father, Miss Birling?
The Inspector's questioning of Sheila is completed and he now turns his attention to her father. Priestley cleverly uses this as a device to clear the stage of everyone except for Sheila and Gerald, as the Inspector goes with Eric to find Mr Birling. This neat piece of writing allows Priestley to build up the tension at the end of the act, by having Gerald ask Sheila to keep a secret from the Inspector. She refuses, and when the Inspector returns his single remark, 'Well?', that is all that is needed to leave the audience waiting in anticipation as the curtain falls on Act One.

Notice how, with the Inspector out of the room, Sheila takes over his role by interrogating Gerald, who comes out of it badly. This is a part which Sheila plays consistently, after her own confession.

47/49	Lies
45/56	Power
31/56	Status
46/49	Sheila
39/49	Gerald

---

49 SHEILA: Oh don't be stupid. We haven't much time.
Sheila confronts Gerald with his dishonesty just as the Inspector would have done. She even uses much the same words. Interestingly, she also echoes the Inspector's comment about not having much time. In spite of Gerald's reluctance to reply, her barrage of questions seem to answer themselves. Like the Inspector, she *knows*. Priestley handles the dialogue so well, and uses the silence of the characters so skilfully, that we, too, feel that we know the answers to many of the questions which are asked in the play, the moment they are spoken.

48/50	Lies
48/52	Sheila
48/52	Gerald
47/53	The Inspector

---

50 INSPECTOR: Well?
By the end of Act One the general development and style of the play have become clear. However, Priestley has written the play in such a way that each of the three acts contains surprises for the audience, and there are twists and turns right up to the end.

49/51	Lies

Act 2

The Inspector begins to question Gerald

51 INSPECTOR [*to* GERALD]: **Well?**
As with Act Three, Priestley begins this act at the same moment as the previous one ended. The division of the acts therefore serves no real dramatic purpose; this is Priestley's way of overcoming the forced break in the action in the theatre. Act Two follows the same pattern as the first, in that two characters are interrogated – this time it is the turn of Gerald and Mrs Birling. In the final act the pattern continues, except that Eric is questioned and then, in his absence, so is the Inspector. In all three acts we see one character who is resistant to questioning and one who is not.

50/53	Lies
47/54	Remorse

52 GERALD [*with an effort*]: **Inspector, I think Miss Birling . . .**
Notice how Gerald echoes the concern of Mr Birling to keep Sheila away from anything 'unpleasant'. Is this because he cares for her and does not wish to upset her? Or is it because he thinks of himself as superior to her, and is therefore being condescending?

34/55	Love
49/54	Sheila
49/53	Gerald

53 INSPECTOR: And you think young women ought to . . .
The Inspector exposes Gerald's hypocrisy by turning his own words against him. This is characteristic of the Inspector's questioning-technique. Not only does he turn each character's words back upon them, but their actions also. This reversal of things, the revealing of the opposite sides of things, and the turning upside down of people's worlds, runs throughout the structure of the play.

51/57	Lies
45/54	Responsibility
52/54	Gerald
49/55	The Inspector

54 GERALD: I neither said that nor even . . .
Gerald protests that he did not imply that Sheila was being selfish or vindictive. Do you believe him?

Notice how it is Sheila who accuses herself of these things, probably because she has been made to recognize that she does in fact possess these characteristics. Was it her intention to take pleasure in watching Gerald be 'put through it', do you think? Is this the reason why she said that 'it might be better' for her? What other reason could Sheila have for wanting to stay, which might make her feel better afterwards? (Remember what the Inspector said to her immediately after she had said that she was 'really responsible' at the end of the last act.)

51/58	Remorse
53/55	Responsibility
52/55	Sheila
53/64	Gerald

55 INSPECTOR [*sternly to them both*]: **You see, we . . .**
The Inspector makes one of his un-policemanlike comments, which emphasizes for Sheila how strange he seems: 'I don't understand about you.' The Inspector seems to imply that people should be sharing their innocence and love, but if there is neither of these, they must share whatever other characteristics they have. At the end of the play we see how Sheila and Eric share a common view which divides them from the others, who share opposite attitudes towards what has happened.

52/57	Love
54/63	Responsibility
54/56	Sheila
35/61	Eric
53/56	The Inspector

There is another implication in the Inspector's comment. The society in which the Birlings live has shared out its material riches very unequally. This is made plain at several points in the play, and students should have no difficulty in picking out good examples. Although some people, like the Birlings and Gerald, have been granted a lion's share of the material riches of their society, the same people are extremely reluctant to accept a similar-sized share of the responsibility for those who have been less generously treated. In fact, they seem to want to avoid all such responsibility. The Inspector points out that if this is the case, then what will have to be shared out is guilt and blame.

The Inspector's message would have seemed very appropriate to audiences in 1945 and 1946. They were emerging from six years of terrible warfare, and were very concerned with questions about what kind of a world they should be striving to produce. The central question of the play is whether Eva Smith's fate was mainly a result of the kind of society which existed in 1912, or was mainly a result of unchangeable human nature. The fact that *some* characters in the play give us hope that they are able to learn and to change themselves strongly suggests the answer to Priestley's question.

Sheila sees something 'special' about the Inspector

56 INSPECTOR [*calmly*]: **There's no reason why you should.**
The Inspector looks back at Sheila calmly as she stares wonderingly at him. We sense that some kind of rapport, or understanding, now exists between them which was not there before. No words are spoken to suggest that this is the case; we just feel that this is what has happened. By using this kind of technique, Priestley involves the audience more with the characters. We feel that we know them, and they seem more 'alive'. We also make guesses about what the characters are feeling and thinking, as here. This encourages us to identify with some characters more than with others, and therefore to take sides in the arguments which they have and over the opinions they express.

48/60	Power
48/57	Status
55/57	Sheila
55/58	The Inspector

Mrs Birling returns

57 SHEILA: You see, I feel you're . . .
Sheila tries to warn her mother that the more she puts on airs and graces, the worse it will be for her eventually. How believable do you find Mrs Birling's reply, that she does not know what her daughter is talking about? It becomes clear that this is a typical reaction from Mrs Birling. The Inspector comments that the 'young ones' are more impressionable, which emphasizes our feeling that Mrs Birling's attitudes are too hard-set to be changed by anything. Notice how she attempts to send her daughter to bed like a naughty
child.

53/59	Lies
55/68	Love
44/59	Pride
56/59	Status
43/58	Mrs Birling
56/59	Sheila

58 INSPECTOR [*coolly*]: **We often do on the young . . .**
The Inspector uses the word 'impressionable'. Look carefully at how Mrs Birling responds to the Inspector's comment. Do you think that she understands what he is implying? Notice how Priestley makes this clear to the audience in his stage-directions at this point. What *is* the Inspector implying here, do you think?

54/69	Remorse
57/59	Mrs Birling
56/60	The Inspector

Characters and ideas previous/next comment

Act 2

59 SHEILA: I don't know. Perhaps it's because . . .
Sheila is beginning to see through the veil of respectability which her mother surrounds herself with. The essential foolishness of the pretence is identified here for us. Mrs Birling's use of language – 'impertinent' – and the way it is wholly out of place, is developed by Priestley when he makes the Inspector draw attention to another inappropriate word – 'offence'. Priestley's use of dialogue shows us how Mrs Birling both reveals the truth about herself, and condemns herself at the same time, by the words which come out of her mouth.

57/61	Lies
57/62	Pride
57/60	Status
58/60	Mrs Birling
57/60	Sheila

60 MRS BIRLING [*rebuking them*]: I'm talking to the Inspector . . .
Mrs Birling ignores the warnings from Sheila and presses on regardless with her snobbish attempts to intimidate the Inspector. She uses her husband's status to try to gain an advantage. She has already attempted to discount Eva as one of the 'girls of that class', and has criticized the Inspector for his 'impertinent' attitude. She attempts to put everyone else in the position of children and herself in the position of parent. In this way she can feel superior. This tells us just as much about Mrs Birling's attitude to other people in general as it does about her conduct as a parent.

56/65	Power
59/65	Status
59/61	Mrs Birling
59/62	Sheila
58/62	The Inspector

61 MRS BIRLING: No, of course not. He's only . . .
Mrs Birling makes two completely erroneous statements about Eric's drinking and his maturity. This marks the beginning of the undermining of her complacency.

59/62	Lies
60/62	Mrs Birling
55/63	Eric

Eric is exposed as a drunkard

62 MRS BIRLING: But it's you – and not the Inspector . . .
Mrs Birling is very put out by the way it is Sheila, and not the Inspector, who is revealing all the embarrassing truths. This is important, and Mrs Birling is quite correct. Although we sense that the Inspector actually knows a lot more than he lets on, he usually works by putting characters in a position where they admit the truth of what they have done, rather than by directly accusing them of things.

61/63	Lies
59/77	Pride
61/65	Mrs Birling
60/63	Sheila
60/63	The Inspector

63 SHEILA [*rather wildly, with laugh*]: No, he's giving us . . .
Sheila completes the popular adage about giving people enough rope. The Inspector is beginning to take over completely: notice how he has countermanded Mr Birling's instructions about Eric going to bed. Shortly he does the same about letting Eric have a drink. The important thing, of course, is the way both Sheila and Eric now begin to take much more notice of the Inspector than of their own parents. Why do they behave in this way?

62/64	Lies
55/65	Responsibility
62/70	Sheila
61/84	Eric
62/74	The Inspector

64 GERALD: I didn't propose to stay long . . .
What was Gerald doing in a bar which, as he admits himself, was the known haunt of prostitutes and their clients? Is this another example of the hypocrisy of Gerald?

63/65	Lies
54/65	Gerald

We learn of Gerald and the girl

65 GERALD: Of course I do. . . .
Ironically, Gerald describes his behaviour in snatching the girl away from the clutches of Joe Meggarty – whom he here describes as 'a notorious womanizer as well as being one of the worst sots and rogues in Brumley' – as though he were conducting some kind of rescue mission. Given the way he subsequently uses the girl and then discards her when he has finished with her, because her presence becomes rather inconvenient, we might wonder how different Gerald and Joe Meggarty really are.

Although Mrs Birling appears shocked to learn of the commonly accepted truth about Joe Meggarty, we should be cautious. Is it credible that she can have been so ignorant of the man's public reputation if at least three of the six people present took it as a matter of common knowledge?

Notice how, as the play progresses, it is the supposedly honourable members of the local community who, one by one, are held up and stripped of their smug and self-congratulatory veneer of respectability. By the time the play is concluded, the behaviour and basic moral values have been thoroughly discredited of the following prominent public figures: a local Alderman, ex-Lord Mayor and successful businessman; the son of an ex-Lord Mayor; another Alderman; the son of local gentry; and the chair of the Brumley Women's Charity Organization. What does this lead you to suspect about the basic values of the society in which these people have been able to rise to such high positions? This is the question which Priestley has put at the centre of his play, and which he intended to leave at the forefront of his audience's minds as they left the theatre.

Characters and ideas previous/next comment

64/66	Lies
60/69	Power
63/68	Responsibility
60/66	Status
62/66	Mrs Birling
64/67	Gerald

---

66 MRS BIRLING [*staggered*]: Well, really! Alderman Meggarty! . . .
People like the Birlings have pretensions to superiority over other people, as do those they mix with. This superiority is not just a matter of wealth or material possessions, it embraces moral and general values as human beings. Mrs Birling's attitude towards the Eva Smiths of this world – 'girls of that class' – reflects her feelings that she is essentially a better human being than they are, and is not just an observation that she is wealthier.

One of the main buttresses for the Birlings' snobbery is that they mix with other people like themselves. This is what shocks Mrs Birling about the revelations concerning Alderman Meggarty. This is the other side of respectability. Later we learn that Gerald Croft and Eric are not so dissimilar to Meggarty in their attitudes towards women. The other characters are revealed as being little better.

The play is set in an age when very high standards were expected from public figures, and when the punishment for those who failed to live up to them – the 'scandal' which so terrifies Birling – was much harsher than is the case today.

However, even today we expect public figures to live by higher standards than we tend to apply to other people. Do you think this is hypocritical of us? If you do, think carefully about your feelings towards the characters in the play, and try to decide how much hypocrisy is creeping into your own views. For example, are you glad when, at the end of the play, it looks as though Gerald and Mr and Mrs Birling are really going to get their come-uppance? Do you find the behaviour and reputation of Joe Meggarty any more offensive than that of Eric, or of Gerald?

65/67	Lies
65/77	Status
65/71	Mrs Birling

Now work the exercise the other way around. Try to recall some prominent scandals which have happened in recent years involving well-known people. Look at how the newspapers and other media treated the misdemeanours of these people. Was the treatment of the people involved mainly determined by what they did, or by the fact that they were well known? There are probably many people who have done things equally reprehensible, but whom the media took no interest in. How fair is this? What do you think the Inspector would have said about this state of affairs?

---

67 GERALD: Yes. I asked her questions about herself. . . .
Gerald tells his story at considerable length. The few interruptions he does get are probably dramatically necessary, to stop his speech becoming a very long monologue. He fills in a considerable amount of background on the girl.

The girl's account of the factory and the shop were, as Gerald says, 'deliberately vague'. This is a clever piece of plot construction on Priestley's part, because this vagueness allows the characters at the end of the play to try to pretend that several different girls were involved, although this seems rather unlikely. However, this skilful touch does allow Priestley to avoid any definite identification of the girl, or girls.

66/68	Lies
65/68	Gerald

---

68 GERALD [*steadily*]: I discovered, not that night but . . .
Gerald explains that he deliberately met the girl a second time. His comment that he 'didn't like the idea of her going back to the Palace bar' suggests that if he had not set the girl up in Charlie Brunswick's rooms, she would have returned to what he has already called the 'favourite haunt of women of the town'. In other words, he was rescuing her from prostitution. Ironically, his actions reduced her to little else, as did those of Eric later.

We are not told whether the girl agreed to meet Gerald, or whether she was a willing partner in his bed. We are told that she felt 'grateful' to him, but this is explained as only natural, under the circumstances. To what extent, therefore, can we feel that Eva Smith was in some ways responsible for her own tragedy? After all, she did not have to go on strike, any more than she had to accept Gerald's offer of rooms, or go to the Palace bar, or let Eric take her home. Or is this an unreasonable attitude for us to adopt towards Eva?

67/69	Lies
57/69	Love
65/69	Responsibility
67/69	Gerald

---

69 BIRLING [*rather taken aback*]: Well, I only did . . .
Mr Birling goes on to say that he dislikes the way his daughter, 'a young unmarried girl', is being dragged into the affair. Birling's hypocrisy is staggering. His description of his own daughter perfectly sums up the situation of Eva Smith, but he adopts entirely different standards when considering her. We can recall that Gerald, too, did not want Sheila to hear him being interrogated by the Inspector a little earlier in this act. Gerald may well have wanted to save himself embarrassment, but he also clearly wanted to protect Sheila from unpleasantness.

Both Birling and Gerald have completely different standards which they apply to women of different class. Earlier, in Act One, we saw how they joked about the 'fun' that young men get up to. A great deal of their manner seems to be based upon the 'boys-will-be-boys' view of sexual relationships. Gerald used the girl and then discarded her, just as Birling did. Eric abused the girl sexually and treated her, as the Inspector says in Act Three, 'as if she was an animal, a thing, not a person'.

68/70	Lies
68/79	Love
65/75	Power
58/70	Remorse
68/71	Responsibility
45/75	Birling
68/70	Gerald

Sheila returns the ring to Gerald   41

Characters and ideas previous/next comment

The society which Priestley has set his play in, was, by our standards, very repressive about sexual matters, and also hypocritically sensitive about their being discussed.

70 SHEILA: **Yes, and it was I who had . . .**
Sheila refuses to be treated like a child any longer. She rebels against her father's attempt to cut her out of the conversation. Notice how her sharp inquisitive tone forces Gerald to admit the truth to himself. The process is shown as being painful but necessary: as Sheila says, 'I've a right to know.' The suggestion is that each of us has a similar right to know the truth about ourselves. Gerald owes it to *himself* to tell the truth.

69/71	Lies
69/72	Remorse
63/73	Sheila
69/72	Gerald

71 MRS BIRLING: **It's disgusting to me.**
What exactly is Mrs Birling disgusted about? Why is she not equally disgusted when her son's treatment of Eva Smith is revealed? Or is it not really what has been *done* by people that disgusts her? What else could it be?

70/72	Lies
69/73	Responsibility
66/76	Mrs Birling

Sheila returns the ring to Gerald

72 GERALD: **I see. Well, I was expecting this.**
Why was Gerald expecting Sheila to give him his ring back? It certainly cannot be because of what he has done, because he knew all about that before he ever gave her the ring in the first place. So what do you think is the real reason?

Look carefully at what Gerald says. Do you think he feels ashamed of what he has done? Do you think he felt ashamed whilst the Inspector was questioning him?

71/73	Lies
70/73	Remorse
70/73	Gerald

73 SHEILA: **I don't dislike you as I did . . .**
Sheila hands back to Gerald the engagement ring which at the start of the play she said she would never let out of her sight for an instant. This is another of the play's many reversals and contrasts.

Sheila is scrupulously fair. Notice how she gives Gerald credit for his honesty, and how she accepts that he acted out of honourable motives when he first became involved with the girl. She even accepts that the whole thing was partly her own fault, because of the state the girl was in when she met up with Gerald. She does not reject Gerald permanently, but says that what has happened has made a difference; they are not the same people who sat down to dinner earlier that evening, and that they will have to 'start all over again'. This kind of thorough honesty is noticeably lacking in the other characters.

72/76	Lies
72/78	Remorse
71/75	Responsibility
70/75	Sheila
72/74	Gerald

Gerald goes for a walk

74 GERALD: **I don't think so. Excuse me.**
Do you think that the Inspector makes much of an impression upon Gerald? It seems likely from what happens in the next act that Eric will probably not become the same sort of hard-headed businessman as his father; but do you think that Gerald probably will?

With this line, Gerald goes out. We do not encounter him again until the second half of Act Three. Priestley manipulates the entrances and exits of

73/80	Gerald
63/75	The Inspector

characters very skilfully. Notice how Priestley uses Gerald's absence to reveal certain things about the Birlings, which they are then keen to keep hidden at the end of Act Three, when he returns. The same technique is used whenever a character is out of the room, to develop the story so that when they return some kind of revelation can be made to them. Often this produces feelings of shock from them, as when Eric almost attacks his mother when he learns what we already have been told about her refusal to help Eva.

The structure of *An Inspector Calls* is very well crafted. Priestley uses events, characters and the ordering of the play's many incidents to sustain the audience's fascination and sense of anticipation. Priestley also makes considerable use of contrasts of mood and speed, switching from the complacency of the characters at the opening to their general anxiety and then terror. He then allows the family to sink partially back into their complacent mood by offering them the 'get-out' of a moral safety-net – everything has been a hoax – and then startles and delights the audience by snatching their security away in the last few seconds of the play.

Mrs Birling is shown a photograph

75 INSPECTOR [*massively*]: Public men, Mr Birling, have responsibilities . . .
Mr Birling's response to this self-evident truth is astounding: 'possibly', he says. This prefaces a long speech by Sheila in which she spells out what has happened so far in the play. In this respect she is acting, as the Inspector sometimes does, like the chorus in a Greek tragedy. Priestley never seems to let this become obtrusive, however, or sound like somebody delivering a sermon of some kind. Look closely at Sheila's speech. Can you see how a realistic effect has been achieved here? (Look at the conversational tone, and the 'natural' language).

69/87	Power
73/80	Responsibility
69/81	Birling
73/79	Sheila
74/76	The Inspector

76 INSPECTOR: Yes, a very good reason. You'll remember . . .
The Inspector forces Mrs Birling to admit to her part in the fate of the girl only with difficulty, and only after she has lied about knowing the girl. Notice how the Inspector uses the name Eva Smith and Mrs Birling agrees that she had seen her. This is interesting, because Mrs Birling goes on to confirm that the girl did not use the name Eva Smith, or even Daisy Renton, but called herself 'Mrs Birling'.

73/77	Lies
71/77	Mrs Birling
75/78	The Inspector

No one notices that the identification of the girl whom Mrs Birling saw, as Daisy Renton and Eva Smith, rests entirely upon the Inspector's say-so. The Inspector shows a photograph on only three occasions, and to three separate people: to Mr Birling, Sheila and Mrs Birling. This is important in Act Three, because it allows for the possibility that different photographs were used, and therefore different girls were involved.

We learn of Mrs Birling and the girl

77 MRS BIRLING [*stung*]: Yes, it was. . . .
This is the key to Mrs Birling's attitude towards the girl. Mrs Birling had not felt that the girl had been respectful enough towards her. She felt that the girl was 'getting above herself' and, presumably, decided to 'take her down a peg or two' in consequence. Notice how Mrs Birling prides herself on being a good judge of character. She says that it did not take her long to get 'the truth – or some of the truth' out of her.

76/78	Lies
62/87	Pride
66/81	Status
76/78	Mrs Birling

Characters and ideas previous/next comment

Whilst Mrs Birling feels that it was important to get at what she saw as the truth about the girl, here we see her as extremely reluctant to do the same in her own case. She deeply resents the Inspector as he gets the truth – or some of it – out of other people in short order.

78 MRS BIRLING: If you think you can bring . . .
Mrs Birling is confident that she can resist the Inspector's questioning. She is convinced that she has done nothing wrong. Does the Inspector ever manage to dislodge her from this view, do you think? Given Mrs Birling's very strong stand against him, how *does* the Inspector manage successfully to get her to talk about her part in the whole affair?

77/83	Lies
73/79	Remorse
77/82	Mrs Birling
76/83	The Inspector

We learn of the dead girl's pregnancy

79 INSPECTOR [*very deliberately*]: Then the next time . . .
The Inspector drops another bombshell by revealing that the dead girl was pregnant. This increases our feelings of sympathy for the dead girl, and outrages Sheila. But is Priestley going rather 'over the top' here? In Act Three we hear Eric ask Mr Birling not to 'pile it on', and during his own writing career, Priestley was sometimes accused of 'loading the dice' and 'piling on the agony' in his works. How justified do you think this criticism is when applied to *An Inspector Calls*?

69/81	Love
78/83	Remorse
75/81	Sheila

80 BIRLING: Look here, this wasn't Gerald Croft –
Notice how this suspicion is raised and squashed at once. Priestley wants the audience to question the motives of the characters in the play. He also wants the audience to examine their own feelings about what has happened to Eva Smith. But Priestley skilfully prevents people travelling up blind alleys. What advantages are gained by ruling out Gerald Croft as a candidate for being the father of Eva's child, therefore? How would the dramatic structure have been blurred and weakened by leaving this question unasked, and unanswered?

75/82	Responsibility
74/82	Gerald

81 SHEILA [*with feeling*]: Mother, I think it was cruel . . .
Notice how different the reactions of Sheila and her father are here. Sheila denounces the action for what it was, whilst Birling thinks only of the possible scandal if the Press should take up the story. The two reactions are revealing in what they identify as the main concerns and priorities of the two characters concerned.

79/82	Love
77/109	Status
75/82	Birling
79/91	Sheila

82 MRS BIRLING: Whatever it was, I know . . .
Mrs Birling uses the same phrase which the Inspector will use in a moment – she lost 'all patience' with the girl. The irony, of course, is that it was the girl who actually showed fine feelings of tact and delicacy by protecting Eric. Mrs Birling on the other hand displayed arrogance, intolerance and snobbery. She dismissed the feelings of her social inferior, just as her husband showed indifference to the fate of his sacked factory girl.

81/84	Love
80/84	Responsibility
81/94	Birling
78/83	Mrs Birling
80/93	Gerald

The Birlings are wholly unsympathetic, and Priestley has so constructed their characters that it is impossible for us to feel any sympathy for their final predicament. Quite the reverse, in fact; we perhaps tend to feel that they get their deserved come-uppance. Notice how this is very different to the way we are encouraged to feel about Eric or Sheila. But this contrast between the attitudes of the young and old is tempered by Priestley's inclusion of the character of Gerald.

Notice how, dramatically speaking, Gerald is a more complicated character than most of the others. His function at different times is to side with the Birlings, act as a contrast to both 'sides' of the family in some way or other, represent the 'real' upper class, as opposed to the social-climbers, fill in narrative background on the girl, and supply plausible-sounding explanations at the end of the play.

83 INSPECTOR [*sternly*]: **I warn you, you're making . . .**
The Inspector was helpful and gentle towards Sheila, because she admitted to her part in things at once and was genuinely concerned about the girl. Mrs Birling is much more hard-faced and hard-hearted, and so the Inspector gives her a much rougher time of things. Notice how he hounds Mrs Birling during these exchanges.

78/84	Lies
79/99	Remorse
82/84	Mrs Birling
78/86	The Inspector

Mrs Birling blames the baby's father

84 MRS BIRLING: **Then he'd be entirely responsible– . . .**
As the Inspector interviews different characters in each act, we come to see the scale of the 'offence' each has committed increasing with every turn. Here Mrs Birling identifies the one who she thinks is most to blame, the one with the greatest responsibility in the whole affair. She is as blind to the irony of what she is saying as she has been to everything else around her; her son's drinking, the behaviour of so-called respectable figures of the community, and so on up to the 'real' family life which surrounds her. Just as her rejection of the pregnant girl was a kind of death-sentence for her grandchild, so here her condemnation of the father is a kind of ultimate judgement upon her own son.

83/87	Lies
82/93	Love
82/85	Responsibility
83/85	Mrs Birling
63/87	Eric

85 MRS BIRLING [*triumphantly*]: **I'm glad to hear it.**
Mrs Birling has finally got herself off the hook and landed the Inspector on it. Now he will have to go away, do his duty, and get on with his job. He will stop bothering the Birling family and take his unpleasant manner away with him. Mrs Birling is, perhaps understandably, triumphant.

Almost exactly as in the situation which occurs at the end of the play, Priestley allows a false sense of security to develop, before smashing it to pieces. The difference here, of course, is that the audience, largely thanks to Sheila, have seen the blow descending. This is a classic technique of the 'suspense' writer, where the audience feels the urge to shout 'look out behind you!'. Here the threat is not behind Mr and Mrs Birling, but has been right under their noses all along.

Notice how Priestley changes the way he uses this technique at the end of the play, where the audience are also kept in the dark about what will happen, and therefore share the characters' sense of surprise.

84/86	Responsibility
84/86	Mrs Birling

86 MRS BIRLING: **Waiting for what?**
Mrs Birling asks the Inspector the fatal question. Both Sheila and the audience are aware by now of the answer which will be coming in reply, and we wait for the bombshell to drop. Priestley's use of dramatic surprises and

85/95	Responsibility
85/87	Mrs Birling
83/88	The Inspector

reversals like this is a technique which puts great sparkle into the action of the play.

Sudden contrasts of mood and character fill the drama, and the author's use of irony and dramatic tension – as here, when we know what is coming but the character concerned does not – keep the audience in a state of permanent anticipation. Priestley uses this technique with the deceptive ease of a master craftsman. In fact it is a notoriously difficult effect to achieve without it degenerating into the obvious and the contrived.

Notice how, right at the very end of the act and with great skill, Priestley uses the simple device of the Inspector holding up his hand to focus all the tension into the silence, as Eric enters and the curtain falls.

Eric is exposed as the father

87 MRS BIRLING [*agitated*]: I don't believe it. I *won't* . . .
Mrs Birling finally realizes the truth of what has been revealed. Notice how she decides whether or not she will believe things, not on the basis of whether they are *true*, but on the basis of whether she finds the truth attractive or palatable. Her attitude conveniently allows her to banish those things which she finds unpleasant. Reality, for Mrs Birling, must accord with her own cosy world before it can be acknowledged. She reserves the right to decide what reality is.

84/91	Lies
75/92	Power
77/112	Pride
86/94	Mrs Birling
84/90	Eric

Looking back over this act, would you say that Mrs Birling is completely unpleasant? Are we unable to feel any sympathy for her? The ending of the act has revealed her as a morally weak woman, unable to cope with the real world. We might feel able to pity her weakness, were it not for the fact that her social position has enabled her to inflict such damage on the lives of others. Has she *any* redeeming features?

88 [INSPECTOR *holds up a hand. We hear the front door. . . .*]
Since the action of the play, as Priestley says at the start, is 'continuous', what is the point of bringing down the curtain and splitting up the action into three chunks in the way he has? What dramatic effect does Priestley achieve by doing this, which would have been impossible otherwise?

| 86/89 | The Inspector |

Characters and ideas previous/next comment

Act 3

89 *Exactly as at the end of Act Two.*
An Inspector Calls is a play in which the author has kept the story of the drama in one place – the Birling's dining room – the action of the drama straightforward without any complicating sub-plots, and the passing of time the same as in the theatre: that is, the events depicted in the play actually take up about the same amount of time as passes in the theatre. There are no jumps in time – like 'flashbacks', for example – there are no shifts in setting, and the story is about one thing only. The breaks between acts are, as here, not allowed to disturb the action of the play and are not used to shift setting. This makes the action of the play very realistic and convincing, concentrating the attention of the audience and making the ending all the more startling.

In ancient times it was thought that a good play kept the place, action and time together, in this very compact way. Keeping these three aspects of the play unified like this was thought to make a good structure for a play, and a playwright who did this was said to be keeping to the 'three unities'. We can see how Priestley has produced a textbook example of how to do this. Our attention is completely concentrated on what happens, and nothing at all is allowed to distract us.

Notice how everything which actually happened to Eva Smith is described, or reported, to us. All the actual action of the strike and sackings, the pick-up in the Palace Bar, the 'love-nest' in Charlie Brunswick's rooms, the rape by Eric, and the interview with Mrs Birling, all these things happen 'off stage'. We are told about them, of course, but we never actually see anything of them. In this sense the Inspector acts rather like a chorus, or reporter. He sums up what has happened at various times, and explains to everyone what they should be learning from the things which have happened. This does of course include us, the audience, who can see our own faults echoed in the play's characters. This was another very old dramatic tradition which was thought to make for a good play. Think carefully: do you agree with this? Would it have made the play more or less effective if we had actually met Eva Smith, actually seen the things which happened to her? Would it have made any difference at all to the impact of what the Inspector says? Would we still have needed the Inspector at all and, if not, could we still be sure that the lessons of the play would have been seen by everyone?

88/100   The Inspector

Eric comes in

90 ERIC: **You know, don't you?**
This comment of Eric's might equally well be addressed to the audience, as to the characters on stage; but Priestley has a few surprises up his sleeve yet for all of us. By now we suspect that this may be the case, and so Eric's comment, as addressed to the audience, is tantalizing. Throughout the play, Priestley has half-involved the audience in a kind of conspiracy – letting them in on a secret and watching the effect of it on some unsuspecting character – and has then sprung startling surprises on characters and audience alike.

Why does Priestley save Eric until last? Up until he got to Mrs Birling, the Inspector had dealt with each character's involvement in the life of Eva Smith in strict chronological order: Birling, then Sheila, then Gerald. The

87/91   Eric

sudden switch of order is completely deliberate on the part of the dramatist. How would the climax of the play have been changed if the Inspector had dealt with Eric and finally Mrs Birling? Where would Eric's verbal attack on his mother then have had to go – at the start of the act, or where Priestley has actually placed it? If you had been the writer of the play, which arrangement do you consider would have produced the best climax for the action of the play?

91 SHEILA: **No, that's not fair, Eric. . . .**
Sheila is now honest enough to have no hesitation in admitting to Eric that she was the one who told their mother about his drunkenness. But she is also fair-minded enough to see that honesty goes both ways, and she refuses to let Eric escape without acknowledging that she protected him for a considerable time. She is not prepared to allow herself to become a scapegoat.

87/93	Lies
81/94	Sheila
90/92	Eric

We learn of Eric and the girl

92 ERIC: **In the Palace bar. I'd been . . .**
We begin to see how Eric is in danger of becoming a younger version of Alderman Joe Meggarty. Notice how he imposed himself on the girl in a similar way and, although he did not tear her blouse as Sheila has told us Meggarty is prone to with young women, he threatened her with violence just the same.

87/93	Power
91/93	Eric

93 INSPECTOR: **And you made love again?**
The Inspector's question produces an interesting answer from Eric. The girl was 'a good sport' and he 'liked her', although he didn't love her 'or anything'. Does this remind you of anything? Compare Eric's relationship with the girl to Gerald's. Compare the words they use when talking about the way their respective relationships developed from the level of conversation to something much more intimate.

91/94	Lies
84/94	Love
92/94	Power
92/94	Eric
82/113	Gerald

94 ERIC: **Well, I'm old enough to be married, . . .**
Eric complains about the way he is being criticized, as though he were a child. Certainly Mr Birling reacts very differently at the news of his son's sexual indiscretions than he did at the news of Gerald's. Notice how the Birlings treat both Eric and Sheila, as though they were still tiny children, ignoring their faults and problems. There is a considerable generation-gap in the Birling household. Eric and Sheila have obviously had expensive educations, material goods and plenty of time to spare. Is there anything which they have not had? How has this contributed to the way they both treated Eva?

Eric's next comment, that he hates 'these fat old tarts round the town – the ones I see some of your respectable friends with –' highlights yet again Birling's double standards. It also suggests that such hypocrisy is fairly widespread among the leading members of local society.

93/95	Lies
93/95	Love
93/96	Power
82/96	Birling
87/99	Mrs Birling
91/108	Sheila
93/95	Eric

95 INSPECTOR: **Did she suggest that you ought to . . .**
In answer to the Inspector's question, we see again that the girl did indeed have the 'fine feelings and scruples' which Mrs Birling denied her in the last

94/96	Lies
94/97	Love

act. The girl obviously had a much clearer sense of moral responsibility than the other people who abused her, ruined her life and drove her to suicide. She would not marry Eric because she knew that he did not love her; she would not take his money because she suspected that he was stealing it. She did not expose him to his mother, because that would have been blackmail.

86/99	Responsibility
94/96	Eric

Eric is exposed as a thief

96 BIRLING [*angrily*]: **What do you mean – *not really*?**
Mr Birling has suddenly acquired a great interest in the precise use of words and in establishing exactly what has gone on. Notice how he is outraged by his son's evasion of the accusation of theft. Eric says that, because he meant to put the money back, it was not really theft. He is unable to suggest how he might have returned the money, but Birling senses correctly that this is immaterial anyway.

By this exchange Priestley has once again highlighted Mr Birling's extreme hypocrisy. When it suits him, he can be as determined as the Inspector to get at the truth, and is equally keen not to mince his words. But of course he does this only when it suits him.

95/97	Lies
94/100	Power
94/97	Birling
95/97	Eric

Sheila and her mother return

97 ERIC: Because you're not the kind of father . . .
With this remark Eric reveals another falsehood in the Birling household, that of the happy family. It would seem that the Birlings are not only callous and unfeeling towards their employees and those whom they perceive as their social inferiors, they are also inadequate as parents. The faults of Eric and Sheila, their weaknesses and temper, can be seen as being largely a result of the way their parents have brought them up.

96/103	Lies
95/99	Love
96/101	Birling
96/98	Eric

98 BIRLING [*angrily*]: **Don't talk to me like that. . . .**
Birling argues that what is really wrong with his son is that he has been spoilt. What precisely does he mean by 'spoilt'? Is he correct, *is* this the trouble with Eric?

97/99	Eric

99 MRS BIRLING [*very distressed now*]: **No – Eric – please – . . .**
Mrs Birling's cries of anguish carry little weight with Eric. His feelings are that she never understands anything and 'never even tried'. This confirms our suspicions that the Birlings are even more to blame for the fate of Eva Smith than we might at first have supposed. They have failed badly in their responsibilities in bringing up their children. Mrs Birling's excuse fails to convince, because we have seen already how she pig-headedly ignores anything which does not suit her cosy view of the world. We can see that Eric is correct in his analysis, and that Mrs Birling is a practised expert at ignoring unpleasant facts, even when they are placed under her nose.

97/102	Love
83/101	Remorse
95/102	Responsibility
94/104	Mrs Birling
98/107	Eric

100 INSPECTOR [*taking charge masterfully*]: **Stop! . . .**
The Inspector begins his summing-up. In the 'trial' of the various characters he has acted at times as the counsel for the defence, counsel for the prosecution, and now he delivers the verdict of the jury. Who plays the part of the judge?

96/102	Power
89/102	The Inspector

101 BIRLING [*unhappily*]: **Look, Inspector—I'd give thousands—...**
Such are the twists of fate. Birling would not pay Eva Smith, a good worker who was about to be promoted to leading operator status, another two shillings and sixpence a week (twelve and a half pence, in decimal currency) for a fair day's work. Now he offers thousands of pounds to undo his mistake. This is the man who prides himself on being such a good, hardheaded businessman. Not only is he offering the money at the wrong time, as the Inspector points out, but from a purely financial point of view he is doing poor business. The sad fact is that Eva probably deserved the extra money anyway—something which Birling never challenges.

99/103	Remorse
97/103	Birling

The Inspector makes a speech—then leaves

102 INSPECTOR: **But just remember this. One Eva Smith . . .**
Inspector Goole's message is that a great wrong has been committed. Although none of the members of the group has committed a crime in the legal sense of the word—apart, perhaps, from Eric—the Inspector has forced them to see that this excuse is simply not good enough. They must do better than simply behave in some kind of 'proper' way, according to some code of 'manners'. Notice the rather biblical sound to the Inspector's words: 'We are members of one body. . . . And I tell you that the time will soon come when, if men will not learn that lesson, then they will be taught it in fire and blood and anguish.' The audiences of 1945 and 1946 would probably also have heard echoes of the famous wartime speeches of Winston Churchill, who tended to use similarly impressive turns of phrase.

99/124	Love
100/109	Power
99/105	Responsibility
100/107	The Inspector

The traditional detective story is a recognized 'type' of literature. A 'type' of literature is sometimes called a *genre* (meaning a kind, a category, or sort). But although *An Inspector Calls* seems to start off like a typical detective story of the 'whodunnit' variety, it soon becomes clear that this is a very strange 'whodunnit' indeed—because *everybody* 'dunnit'. If Priestley had written the play exactly to the formula of the genre, it would probably have been very much less successful. It is because Priestley has gently tricked us at the outset into expecting a typical 'whodunnit', and has then 'broken the rules' in the way he has, that we find the play so fascinating. Like many of the characters and events in the play, the play itself turns out to be something different to what it seemed at first.

Priestley uses several of the standard situations of a 'whodunnit'. There is an investigation into a murder, a limited number of suspects, some false trails, and the murderer is unmasked by a brilliant detective. In a traditional 'whodunnit', the audience's enjoyment would have come from trying to guess who the villain was before the Inspector revealed the answer. But in Priestley's drama we see the circle of guilt widening rather than narrowing, people are drawn *into* the role of villain, rather than excluded from it one by one. This is the reverse of what normally happens.

In *An Inspector Calls* we find actions, which characters have not seen as wrong, revealed as highly immoral by the Inspector, who uncovers the secrets of each character and then shows them how they share part of the responsibility for Eva's death, and therefore part of the guilt. Birling has treated people as cheap labour; Sheila made others suffer because of her childish tantrums; Eric has been a thief and a promiscuous liar; Gerald has lied to his fiancée and 'two-timed' her; and Mrs Birling, Chair of the local charity organization, showed no charity at all. Each character has their excuses torn to shreds by the Inspector, whose questioning, aided by Sheila and Eric's new-found honesty, exposes a tissue of self-deceit. The Inspector makes us see how there are greater criminal acts than those which involve people in breaking the law.

How far can we really accept that Eva Smith, and all the others, were really one and the same person? And how would you counter the suggestion that Eva is too good to be true, that she was too considerate, too kind? Consider each question in turn and try hard to answer them; then see if you can decide whether it actually matters what the answer is for each of them. Would the play work just as well, whatever our answers were?

---

103 BIRLING [*angrily*]: Yes, and you don't realize yet . . .
This accusation is levelled at Eric by Mr Birling. It represents another example of the play's many uses of irony. Of all the people who fail to realize what they have really done, Mr and Mrs Birling are the two clearest examples. All Birling is concerned about is the extent to which things will 'come out', and how much of a scandal there will be.

The Inspector has just left at this point, and does not return. This is the signal for recriminations to break out between the characters. Significantly, it is Mr Birling who kicks off by blaming somebody else – in this case Eric – for everything. We in the audience now have revealed to us the extent to which each character has learned something from the evening's revelations. Much of what we hear is depressing.

97/104	Lies
101/119	Remorse
101/104	Birling

---

104 BIRLING [*angrily*]: Drop that. There's every excuse . . .
Birling is quite correct. We have seen every excuse made in the attempt to justify the actions of Mr and Mrs Birling. Why does Birling not at this stage simply own up to everything? Why do he and his wife still hold on to their blinkered view of things? Who are they trying to convince of their innocence?

103/106	Lies
103/106	Birling
99/112	Mrs Birling

---

105 SHEILA: I don't know where to begin.
Sheila is staggered at her father's 'it turned out unfortunately, that's all –'. Birling's easy dismissal of the events of the night leaves her temporarily floored. But Priestley's point is well made: where *should* Sheila begin? Where should any of us begin, in trying to sort out what to do about a world in which this kind of thing can happen?

Throughout the play we, the audience, might well have had the uncomfortable feeling that the Inspector has not been looking only at the faults of the characters on the stage. Because these faults are so general – greed, pride, lust, and so on – we can see that Priestley's message is directed with equal force at all of us. Notice how each of the characters has made the kinds of excuse that any of us might have been tempted to rely upon, or may already have used in our lives recently: we are 'respectable' and not 'criminals', it 'didn't seem to be anything very terrible at the time', we 'didn't know', we 'didn't understand', our actions were 'justified', we have 'done nothing wrong', we 'did our duty'. The list is long, and all of us can recognize the way people work variations upon just the kinds of weak excuse which the play's characters have offered.

| 102/113 | Responsibility |

---

106 SHEILA: But that's not what I'm talking about.
Sheila says that her parents do not seem to have learned anything from the evening's events. Mr Birling's reply is revealing. He says that he has learned

| 104/108 | Lies |
| 104/109 | Birling |

'plenty'. What do you think he has in mind? How does Birling see the events of the evening?

107 ERIC [*cutting in*]: Yes, and do you remember . . .
For the second time this evening, Eric reminds his father about the pompous and selfish speech he made earlier. This serves the purpose of making a dramatic link between the beginning and the end of the play. It is the completion of Priestley's 'circle', within which the action of the play exists. Notice how this speech of Eric's is also used to allow Sheila to begin wondering aloud about the real identity of the Inspector.

| 99/118 | Eric |
| 102/108 | The Inspector |

Was he really an Inspector?

108 SHEILA: It doesn't much matter now, of course . . .
Alert as ever, it is Sheila who first voices the question which will dominate the rest of the action: '*was* he really a police inspector?' Notice how, unlike everybody else except Eric, she starts from the position that the answer to the question is not really of any importance now. Gerald and Mr and Mrs Birling take the view that nothing else matters apart from this one point.

106/110	Lies
94/115	Sheila
107/109	The Inspector

109 BIRLING: Then look at the way he talked . . .
Birling thinks that it was outrageous of the Inspector to talk to him in the way he did, because of Birling's public position. Yet again, we get the list of public offices trotted out. Birling takes it for granted that these positions confer upon him some kind of special status which means that people must talk to him in a deferential way. In Birling's eyes, the most terrible thing which has happened this evening is that someone has told him to shut up!

102/111	Power
81/112	Status
106/111	Birling
108/110	The Inspector

110 SHEILA: It's all right talking like that now. . . .
Sheila's comment is both accurate and interesting. But exactly *how* did the Inspector make each of them confess? Examine each character's interrogations in turn, and see if you can establish exactly what it was that the Inspector did, in each case, to make them confess.

| 108/113 | Lies |
| 109/113 | The Inspector |

Gerald returns

111 BIRLING: The fact is, you allowed yourselves to . . .
Birling is the one who is bluffing. Look at the way he immediately panics when the doorbell rings. Mrs Birling turns to her husband for decisive action, for leadership, and for authority. She tells Eric and Sheila to 'be quiet'. They are only 'children' and must let their father decide what to do. Look carefully at how Mr Birling reacts to this, and at what he says and does. How misplaced is his wife's confidence in him?

| 109/128 | Power |
| 109/113 | Birling |

112 MRS BIRLING: The rude way he spoke . . .
Mrs Birling is more concerned about the way the Inspector addressed her and her husband, than with the content of what he had to say, or the truth which was revealed. She describes the Inspector's manner as 'extraordinary'. We are led to see that, as far as she is concerned, there was nothing 'extraordinary' at all about her own behaviour, or that of her husband, towards Eva Smith.

87/117	Pride
109/117	Status
104/119	Mrs Birling

Act 3

113 GERALD [*slowly*]: **That man wasn't a police officer.**
Gerald drops his bombshell. This sudden twist in the plot adds a further surprise to those already sprung upon the audience, who by now are probably completely unable to guess what will happen next. Yet again, like a sorcerer, Priestley has transformed the situation into something altogether different, at a single stroke. This is important, because Priestley was working within a known format – the 'whodunnit' – and needed to keep up the momentum of the action, yet also make sure that the play did not become predictable.

Birling feels that this news 'makes all the difference'. Gerald agrees: 'Of course!' Sheila's acid comment cuts them both to the quick: 'I suppose we're all nice people now.'

Dramatically, Gerald's revelation is crucial, because it allows some of the characters the opportunity to think that they are off the hook. In this sense, it is the acid-test of what they have each learned. How each character reacts to the possibility of moral escape tells us everything about their integrity. You should study closely, and note in detail, what each of them does next.

Characters and ideas previous/next comment

110/115	Lies
105/118	Responsibility
111/115	Birling
93/114	Gerald
110/114	The Inspector

114 GERALD: Yes. I met a police sergeant I know . . .
Gerald explains that he has deduced that Inspector Goole is a fake. Writing in January 1947, Sewell Stokes, a contemporary critic, noted wittily that it was no surprise to the audience to know that Inspector Goole did not exist. They had known all the time it was Inspector Priestley. Stokes put his finger on a real danger lurking within *An Inspector Calls* – that it might become a moral lecture by the author. Most modern critics feel that Priestley successfully avoided this danger. What do you think? Can you point to any evidence to support your conclusions?

113/115	Gerald
113/122	The Inspector

There is no 'Inspector Goole'

115 BIRLING [*excitedly*]: **By Jingo! A fake!**
Birling is excited at the prospect that the Inspector was a fake. For him, this changes everything: it cancels out his blame, absolves him of guilt, and renders the entire incident null and void.

Notice the blunt and matter-of-fact words which Birling uses. This is in contrast to the way Sheila speaks about the Inspector, as though he were much more mysterious, spiritual and ephemeral. Birling and Gerald are determined to treat the incident as a hoax, a practical joke. By doing this they can reduce everything which has happened to the level of a stunt or trick. This is the difference between them and Sheila, for she does not see the performance of the Inspector as a sequence of rabbits-out-of-hats and other conjuror's tricks, she sees it as revelation of the real truth.

113/116	Lies
113/117	Birling
108/124	Sheila
114/116	Gerald

116 GERALD: That's all right. I don't want to. . . .
Gerald's attitude is summed up well here. What he seems to want is not the truth, but an explanation. We suspect that, like Birling, he wants the events not only explained but, more importantly, explained away.

115/119	Lies
115/117	Gerald

117 BIRLING [*keenly interested*]: **You are, eh? Good! . . .**
Why should Birling be so very pleased at Gerald's attitude here? Remember, as you consider this, that Birling is very conscious that Gerald and his family are, in Birling's eyes, socially superior to them.

112/124	Pride
112/119	Status
115/119	Birling
116/120	Gerald

118 ERIC: Whoever that chap was, the fact remains . . .
Eric has changed considerably during the course of the play, even during this act. Compare his responsible and adult manner now with that at the start of the act, where he criticized Sheila for revealing the truth about his drunkenness: 'Why, you little sneak!'

| 113/122 | Responsibility |
| 107/123 | Eric |

---

119 BIRLING: Look – for God's sake!
Mr Birling finally loses patience with Sheila's determined attempt to reveal their hypocrisy for what it is. Mrs Birling is outraged by her husband's language: 'Arthur!', she cries. It is a sad reflection on her character that we see her more upset by Birling's swearing than by what she has been told this evening.

116/120	Lies
103/123	Remorse
117/124	Status
117/122	Birling
112/0	Mrs Birling

---

120 GERALD: Did we? Who says so?
Think back across the events of the play and examine Gerald's reasoning here very carefully. Is he right that there *is* 'no more real evidence' that they all drove a girl to commit suicide, than that their visitor was a real police officer?

| 119/121 | Lies |
| 117/121 | Gerald |

Was there more than one girl?

121 GERALD: We've no proof it was the same photograph . . .
Just how desperate the Birlings are to find a way to wriggle out of the truth is shown by their willingness to believe this supposition of Gerald's.

| 120/122 | Lies |
| 120/122 | Gerald |

In fact, Gerald's suggestion is really quite unlikely to be correct. The supposition is that the Inspector had three different photographs, that different girls coincidentally presented themselves to charity, met up with Eric, bumped into Gerald, got sacked by Birling and irritated Sheila, all in the correct sequence, with no awkward overlaps in time; and that all these girls looked sufficiently alike to be confused with each other in verbal descriptions. Further, these girls would all have to have been known to the supposed hoaxer, together with their backgrounds and their involvements with all the play's characters. Compared to the straightforward explanation by the Inspector, this seems a most preposterous set of wild coincidences and unlikely facts.

Mr and Mrs Birling are frantic to find some way of explaining away the life story of Eva Smith so that it leaves them untouched by any blame. Notice carefully, they are not worried about guilt, only about the allocation of blame. Their only concern is to avoid the latter, because they are well-used to shrugging off the former, as Mrs Birling does, by being blind to it.

---

122 GERALD: What girl? There were probably four or five . . .
With this remark, Gerald identifies himself with the attitude of Mr Birling towards the events which have taken place. Even if Gerald were correct, what possible difference would this make? Notice how, for Gerald and Birling, it makes all the difference in the world. What does this reveal about how much Gerald has learned from the Inspector's visit?

121/123	Lies
118/126	Responsibility
119/124	Birling
121/125	Gerald
114/126	The Inspector

The idea that up to five different girls might have been involved, one with each of the play's characters, seems incredible. But equally, it seems fairly unlikely that five people, all connected with the same family, should each have been involved in the way they were with the same girl. The point about this is that, although Priestley sets his play out as though it were realistic, it

Act 3

is in fact more like a fairy-story or a parable – a story with a moral (a lesson) for us all, hidden away inside it.

Because of this it is pointless to worry, as some of the characters do here, about who the Inspector *really* was. Sheila is correct – it does not matter.

---

123 ERIC: That doesn't matter to me. . . .
Eric is unmoved by the complicated explanations which Gerald and Birling are developing. The girl whom he loved is dead; nothing else matters for Eric. At this point, Birling surprises the others by asking whether the girl really *is* dead: 'How do we know she is?'. The story makes another swift change of direction as this startling possibility sinks in. It allows Priestley to build up the hopes of the others to the point where they all pin everything on this one way out. At that instant, Priestley smashes the possibility of escape into a thousand pieces. This raising of false hope is very effective in the drama, and contributes a great deal to the play, which depends upon it completely for the power of its ending.

122/125	Lies
119/124	Remorse
118/125	Eric

---

124 BIRLING: I'm convinced it is. . . .
Notice Birling's reaction. He continues: 'No police inquiry. No one girl that all this happens to. No scandal –.' It is left to Sheila to ask: 'And no suicide?'

This tells us a great deal about the major concerns of these two characters. Sheila is most concerned about the girl and her suicide. She will be overjoyed if it turns out that no pregnant young girl took her own life, because this is what has distressed her most.

But Birling is indifferent to the fate of the girl. If the fate of 'Eva' can be separated out, so that *several* girls were involved, he will feel much better. The fact that, even if this were true, it would still mean that each of the girls really did suffer each of the incidents described, does not worry him. It does not even worry him that it would still mean that there was a pregnant young girl, about the same age as his daughter, dead in the infirmary from an agonizing suicide. All that concerns Birling is the possibility of no scandal.

How plausible is the character of Arthur Birling? Can you *really* believe that anyone could be as selfish, heartless, bigoted and blinkered as this man? Yet Priestley makes him believable; this is a tribute to the skill of the dramatist. Try to decide how he managed it.

Birling's 'believability' as a character is an indictment of society, both past and present. We suspect, only too sadly, that Priestley's caricature continues to be alive and well in the flesh.

102/129	Love
117/0	Pride
123/129	Remorse
119/127	Status
122/126	Birling
115/125	Sheila

---

125 GERALD: Anyway we'll see. [*He goes to telephone* . . .
Gerald has appeared, throughout, as a strong and confident character. Notice, however, that at the end he cannot face reality, and tries hard to wriggle out of his responsibilities for the girl's fate. He also tries to do the same for Mr and Mrs Birling, so that none of them have to face up to the consequences of their actions. Gerald still hopes to become engaged to Sheila, but notice how he sides with the Birlings at the end of the play. Priestley probably had a very specific reason for arranging things in this way. Can you think what it might have been?

In this respect Gerald is in fact not as strong as the seemingly much weaker Eric, who at least accepts honestly the faults in his own behaviour and does not try to pretend that he did not do the things he really did. Inside,

123/126	Lies
124/128	Sheila
123/0	Eric
122/129	Gerald

Characters and ideas previous/next comment

character and surface appearance turn out to be the opposites of each other for these two characters. This is typical of the play. Much of *An Inspector Calls* is to do with revealing that, under the surface, things are very different from the way they seem at first glance.

There is no suicide victim

126 BIRLING [*triumphantly*]**: There you are! Proof positive. . . .**
Birling is triumphant. He goes on to say that 'The whole story's just a lot of moonshine'. Notice how, for Birling, the whole story *can* now be discounted.

How credible was the Inspector, though? And how far can we accept the tale of Eva Smith as believable? Before you decide that the whole story is too far-fetched to be true, consider that there are many happenings in life which would not be accepted as credible, if shown in the theatre!

125/129	Lies
122/128	Responsibility
124/127	Birling
122/128	The Inspector

127 BIRLING [*giving him a drink*]**: Yes, he didn't . . .**
Gerald has been out of the house for a while, to have a 'breather', and has been given some time to think. Birling's use of words is revealing. What sort of person do we normally associate with being 'on the run'?

| 124/0 | Status |
| 126/0 | Birling |

128 SHEILA: No, because I remember what he said, . . .
Sheila echoes the Inspector's threat of 'fire and blood and anguish'. The characters have been given a chance to change their ways, before retribution descends upon them. In the traditional 'whodunnit', the criminal would be arrested and taken away by the Inspector for punishment. Not so here, where all of them must 'remember what he said', must change their ways, must punish themselves by accepting the truth about themselves and each other. The 'criminal' is much easier to spot in Priestley's play than in the classic detective story. Persuading the criminals to take their medicine will be much harder.

111/0	Power
126/130	Responsibility
125/129	Sheila
126/130	The Inspector

Gerald offers Sheila the ring again

129 GERALD: Everything's all right now, Sheila. . . .
Gerald is too keen to assume that things can now return to the way they were before the Inspector called. Notice how his offer to give her the ring repeats an event from the start of the play. Significantly, Sheila refuses him. She will not be repeating her reaction when the ring was first offered at the start of the play.

We then see that another event from the start of the play is about to repeat itself. There is the ringing of a bell – an Inspector will be calling.

126/130	Lies
124/0	Love
124/0	Remorse
128/0	Sheila
125/0	Gerald

The telephone rings – an Inspector is to call

130 BIRLING: That was the police. . . .
The final seconds of the play provide us with the final twist in the plot. Not only does this throw Gerald and Mr and Mrs Birling back into a state of total shock and confusion, it makes a mockery of all the elaborate self-congratulation they have been indulging in. It would be a stony-hearted audience which did not feel a thrill of satisfaction at this moment: the culprits are about to get what they deserve. Similarly, we would have to be

129/0	Lies
128/0	Responsibility
128/0	The Inspector

remarkably insensitive not to feel something for the Birlings, to be able to sympathize with their dilemma, if only for occasional brief moments. This is a considerable achievement on Priestley's part, for there has been little which would encourage us to feel much general sympathy for any of them.

The ending of the play is a stunningly effective dramatic moment. We suddenly reconsider our thoughts about Inspector Goole, who at first seemed like a normal, if extremely skilful and well-informed, policeman, then looked instead as if he might possibly have been a hoaxer instead. As things have turned out, he becomes something rather more mysterious. We might now feel inclined to share Sheila's summary of him to Gerald earlier on: 'He was – frightening'.

The audiences in 1945 and 1946 would have understood that the Inspector was proved correct, that society – like the Birlings – would not learn from its warnings. Remember that the play is set in 1912. The audience can clearly see that time did indeed 'soon come when, if men will not learn that lesson, then they will be taught it in fire and blood and anguish'. Do you think that, on the whole, this makes the play an optimistic play or a pessimistic one?

Characters in the play

Mr Arthur Birling

Mr Birling is a smug and successful factory owner, an ex-Lord Mayor of Brumley and a local magistrate. He is not an especially bad or wicked man, indeed he prides himself on his fairness. He pays his employees no more and no less than the going rate, and he feels that people should take care of their own, mind their own business, and generally look after themselves. He does not seek to punish workers who ask for more money, although he is tough and insensitive about such matters, and he simply turns them down on the grounds that it is his duty to keep costs as low as possible, and keep his prices as high as the market will stand.

Mr Birling has little or no imagination, and can see neither the consequences of his own actions, nor the way events in the larger world are moving. Priestley has him make comments about the future – the *Titanic* being unsinkable; the impossibility of war; and the promise of technology – which would have been believed by many other people in 1912, but which would seem narrow-minded and smug to the play's audience in 1945. Mr Birling can see no reason why people should fight a war, as it would upset the businessmen's quest for profit. It never occurs to him that people might value other things more highly. Priestley thereby creates Mr Birling as a stereotype for his age, and something of a caricature of it. This is true of the other characters in the play also, who are rendered as other, different 'types'. Mr Birling is in fact Priestley's example of the callousness and heartlessness of capitalism. Mr Birling's dismissal of Russia as a nation that would always lag behind the others is doubly ironic, given that the play's first performance was in Russia, and that after the Second World War few in the audience would by then have any reservations about the strength of Russia's industrial and military power.

Birling is proud of his status, which concerns him a great deal; he and his wife set great store by his public offices and privileges. Such things influence Birling's values so much that he feels a little uneasy about Gerald Croft marrying his daughter – he senses that Gerald's parents may feel that their son is marrying 'beneath himself'. This is why the possibility that the events at the end of the play may deprive Birling of his promised knighthood upset him far more than anything else.

Mr Birling and his wife both see themselves as pillars of the community, as upholders of all the 'right' values and as guardians of proper conduct. But both of them are exposed by Priestley as hollow, self-centred and essentially heartless. Both of them initially respond to the Inspector by trying to put him in his place, by emphasizing their own position in society. Both of them deal with the truth by hiding it, or hiding from it. Mr Birling does not want his daughter to hear anything 'indelicate' and Mrs Birling is scandalized by the honest descriptions of a supposedly respectable local Alderman. As Eric points out, his father is useless in a real crisis. At the end of the play it is Gerald who does all the thinking, not Mr Birling.

We see how Birling responds to having his own responsibilities and actions challenged: he accuses others, blusters, 'yammers', and schemes of ways to cover up the whole affair. When he learns of Eric's involvement with the girl, his only concern is to get hold of the accounts which Eric has stolen from, so that he can conceal the thefts. It is plain that his motives are not to protect Eric from being found out, but to protect himself from social scandal. He is prepared to distort or ignore the truth if it will allow his family to go on behaving the way they were before. He is blind to the hypocrisy of this, and indifferent when it is pointed out to him. Just before the end of the play he happily argues that 'the whole thing's different now' and congratulates himself on having avoided a scandal. Provided their public reputation is safe, characters like Mr and Mrs Birling will never change their ways, and it is clear from looking at Gerald that there are plenty more where they came from.

Characters in the play

Mrs Sybil Birling

Mrs Birling has a lot in common with her husband, but she is, if anything, even more hard-faced and arrogant than he. She is introduced to us as his social superior and as a rather cold woman. Her manner indicates that she is very conscious of the social position of people, especially her own. She is offended when her husband expresses approval for the cook in front of guests, as this is 'not done'. She is clearly mistress of the house and someone to be reckoned with, as Mr Birling acknowledges right at the beginning when he is rebuked for talking too much. Her rigid code of what is 'proper' is extremely sensitive to any deviations, especially to what she sees as impertinence, rudeness, or people generally 'getting above' themselves. She is extremely snobbish, and expects others to be respectful towards her, to defer to her opinions and not to upset her. She is always on the alert for any criticism of herself or of the family name. She resents being challenged about what she has done and said, even when she is caught red-handed by the Inspector, telling outright lies. She refuses to accept that she has ever done anything wrong.

Mrs Birling seems genuinely shocked to hear about her son's drink problem, and about Joe Meggarty's licentious reputation, although neither piece of information comes as the slightest surprise to Sheila or Gerald. Her concern – shared by her husband – that Sheila should not be exposed to 'unpleasant' things suggests that she regards her daughter as still very much a child. We wonder whether Mrs Birling is genuinely unaware of what is really going on around her in the world, or is just deliberately blind to what she does not wish to see. She seems to have a cosy and comfortable view of the world, and dislikes this being upset, as when the Inspector identifies her part in the girl's fate. She cannot see how the suicide of a 'lower class' person is of any importance to her or her family.

When exposed to criticism, or whenever she feels otherwise threatened, Mrs Birling retreats behind words like 'respectable', 'duty', and 'deserving'. She seems to feel that she is the only valid judge of what such words shall actually mean. If her own position and status have first been suitably acknowledged by those around her, she can be generous and caring, but otherwise she will take offence at what she sees as the 'impertinence' shown to her, and will turn her back on others, however much in need they are. She thinks that different feelings and different standards of behaviour are appropriate for different classes of people. She was offended by Eva Smith's pleas for help, because the girl was 'giving herself ridiculous airs' and was 'claiming elaborate fine feelings'. Mrs Birling refuses to accept that a girl of that class could ever have such feelings. Her vindictive attitude towards the father of the girl's child changes dramatically when she learns that it is her own son, and this clearly illustrates her extreme hypocrisy. She was quite happy to denounce somebody else if it would somehow excuse her own conduct. She criticizes Mr Birling for starting the whole thing, with much the same intentions.

Mrs Birling prides herself on her aloof and cool manner towards others and gives herself considerable airs and graces. She uses her husband's social position as a kind of club with which to try to beat the Inspector into submission, and does not know how to react when this tactic does not work. Her arrogant pretence that all is well, and that she is the mother of a happy family, is rudely shattered when her own son seems to be on the brink of physically attacking her, and accuses her of murdering his child and its mother: 'You killed them both – damn you, damn you –.' However, when the Inspector has gone, Mrs Birling forcefully criticizes the others for not standing firm against someone who is their social inferior. She clearly demonstrates her distaste for such people and seems to think she is quite literally above them, and even that she and her family are above the law. She argues that if *she* had been present when the Inspector first arrived, she would have dealt with his impertinence severely; but by this time we can clearly see this for the hollow sham that it is.

Mrs Birling's attitude at the end of the play is that everything can now go back to being the way it was before the Inspector arrived. She dismisses the events which have been revealed, as if they never happened. Her attitude to the distress of Sheila and Eric is aloof and haughty: 'They're over-tired. In the morning they'll be as amused as we are.' As the telephone rings, we learn that fate has brought Mrs Birling up sharply, but we suspect that she will behave in no more compassionate or caring a way than she has done so far, and may be much harder to rattle for being forewarned. It seems likely that the Inspector's call has hardened her attitudes even further.

Sheila Birling

Sheila is the daughter of the Birlings who, at the start of the play, becomes engaged to Gerald Croft. She is impressionable, and is deeply affected by the Inspector's revelations. Sheila is the only character, apart from Eric, who gives us any cause for optimism in the play. She has an attractive and essentially honest character, and lacks the cold attitude of her parents. As the play proceeds she sees her father exposed as a hard-hearted and vengeful employer, her fiancé exposed as a liar who has had a 'kept woman', her brother exposed as the father of what would have been an illegitimate child, her mother revealed as callous and vindictive, and herself as a vain and spiteful girl who has contributed to the death of a young mother and her unborn child.

Sheila acts at times almost as an accomplice to the Inspector, in that she tends to continue his criticism of the other characters, even when he leaves the stage. Her parents are not slow to point this out, or to take exception to it as a lack of loyalty. In spite of this, Sheila sees no point in concealing either Eric's drink problem or Joe Meggarty's reputation. In this, Sheila is not being vindictive, as Gerald at first mistakenly thinks, but is simply trying, along with the Inspector, to get at the truth. It is interesting to note that up until the Inspector calls, she too has gone along with the socially accepted blindness to such 'lies' around her, but by the end of the play she has undergone a learning experience which we suspect will make her unlikely to be hypocritical in future. Sheila objects to her parents trying to stifle her from speaking out, or trying to 'protect' her from the unpleasant truth; '. . . I'm not a child, don't forget. I've a right to know.' She is frightened by the attitudes of her parents and of Gerald at the end of the play. She feels that, whilst for a while it seemed as though they were learning something, once they have seen a 'way out' for themselves, their learning has stopped.

Because she is more sensitive and alert than the others, and less blinkered, she is the first to realize what the Inspector is driving at in his interviews with people. She sees how the other characters try to cover up and lie, realizes how ineffective her mother's false manner will prove, and how Gerald's desire to conceal his affair will be ineffective. It is Sheila who first recognizes who the father of the baby is. She realizes that the Inspector *knows* all about them. Similarly, it is Sheila who first begins to wonder who the Inspector really is, both during his interrogations and after he has left. She is also the first to speak out about the way the family dishonestly try to pretend that nothing has happened, at the end of the play.

Sheila's honesty leads her to be over-critical of herself at times. She identifies herself with the dead girl, because they were both pretty, the same age, lively and outgoing. She recognizes that such girls are not, as her father sees them, cheap labour, but are people. She feels sorry for the girl's dismissal from her father's factory. However, it has to be noted that Sheila's spiteful complaint against the girl when she worked at Milwards was probably the least justified action of all of the characters, being a tantrum based completely on her own vanity. Sheila got the girl sacked simply for smiling in what she thought was a critical way. The girl did not even smile at Sheila, but at her shop-assistant colleague, and it is clear that Sheila was simply jealous of her prettiness. The only redeeming feature of Sheila's petty behaviour is that she felt bad about it at the time, regretted it deeply later, and admitted honestly to her share of the responsibility for the girl's fate. Sheila, and to a lesser extent her brother Eric, represent those people in the younger generation whom Priestley hopes will learn enough from events to accept their responsibilities for other people. He hopes that they will be the ones to build a better world, based on less selfish, more positive values than those of their parents.

Eric Birling

Eric is the younger brother of Sheila Birling. but has a more secretive personality. This becomes understandable when we learn that he is a habitual drunkard, the father of what would have been an illegitimate child, a liar, a thief and embezzler, and a general ne'er-do-well. He is steadily revealed as the black sheep of the family.

During the first two acts, Eric functions mainly as an irritant to Mr Birling and his complacent and smug ideas, asking what his father deems to be silly questions. Mr Birling clearly thinks that his son has not benefited from the public school and university education which he has given him. Presumably Eric's expensive education was a calculated move by the father to improve his son's status, rather than to develop his critical approach to life. Mr Birling feels that less criticism and more support are in order when Eric seems to be siding with the Inspector and his sister by arguing that the workers have every right to try for higher wages: 'We try for the highest possible prices. And I don't see why she should have been sacked just because she'd a bit more spirit than the others.'

Eric arouses our curiosity with his sudden guffaw in the first act. This is a possible indication that he is getting drunk, or that he knows something about Gerald, because Sheila has just been giving him a ticking-off for neglecting her in favour of his work. Later, we might wonder how much Eric knew about Gerald's affair with the girl the previous summer, which is one of the main reasons he neglected Sheila. Our curiosity about Eric turns to suspicion when he catches himself in mid-comment later on, where he was about to say something about remembering that women find clothes important, and when he becomes uneasy at the Inspector's visit. We begin to think that Eric is concealing things, that he has secrets which he wishes to keep hidden. Both suspicions are encouraged at this point in the play by Priestley and are, of course, fully justified by what we learn about Eric later on.

Eric seems to be hostile and aggressive towards his parents, especially towards his father, unlike his sister Sheila, whose criticisms seem more balanced and whose motives seem more straightforward. Later on we learn that Eric felt unable to approach his father when he was in trouble. Perhaps this is why Eric resents his father, and possibly explains why he drinks so much, because his father's manner has never been sufficiently gentle and loving. This may be why Eva took pity on Eric at their first meeting. Certainly Eva treated Eric, as he himself admits, as if he were a 'kid', and may have recognized in him a need for affection and love which she also had long felt in need of in her own life.

Eric comes across as a weak and lonely figure, but one who is capable of feeling real emotion for another person. He is more demonstrative than all the other characters, and at the end we see him on the verge of physically attacking his mother in his fury at her lack of charity. In fairness, however, we must remember that he had far more provocation than anyone else, for in his eyes his mother was the murderer of his child and its mother. Equally, we must remember that Eric's personal responsibility in the girl's tragedy was also very great indeed.

At the end, Eric frankly admits his part in the destruction of Eva Smith, and we feel that, along with Sheila, he has learned something from the whole affair, unlike the other characters. Eric understands that '. . . the fact remains that I did what I did'. His parents and Gerald all fail to learn this lesson, but Eric can now see that 'It's still the same rotten story whether it's been told to a police inspector or to somebody else. . . . It's what happened to the girl and what we all did to her that matters.' But Eric's inherent weakness may not allow him to change his ways as easily as his stronger sister. We may feel that, for Eric, the learning process may be more difficult to build upon in the future, for he has a more evasive character than Sheila, and perhaps lacks her ability to face things squarely and deal with them head on.

Gerald Croft

Gerald Croft is the son of Sir George and Lady Croft, who own a rival industrial concern to that of the Birlings. He is the fiancé of Sheila Birling. Mr Birling regards Gerald's family very much as social superiors of his own family. Birling is delighted at the possible merger of the two businesses, which his daughter's marriage to Gerald would eventually produce.

Gerald's outlook on life is similar to that of Birling, and he agrees with the way the dismissal of Eva Smith was handled: 'You couldn't have done anything else.' Gerald's vision of the future seems to accord fairly closely with that of Mr Birling, although it is perhaps not quite so self-satisfied and smug.

Like Mr and Mrs Birling, Gerald's first response to his part in the affair of the girl is to attempt to conceal it; but unlike them, he shows genuine remorse when the news of her death finally sinks in. Gerald is also unlike them, in that he seems far less preoccupied with social status or worried about scandal. It is of course possible that his greater social status means that he does not need to be so conscious of status, and that his more privileged position may protect him more from scandal. However, in fairness to Gerald, it becomes clear that he helped Eva out of genuinely humane feelings for her situation. His later involvement with her, however understandable and predictable with the benefit of hindsight, was not premeditated. Neither did he take advantage of her in the violent drunken way in which Eric did and, unlike Eric, he made her genuinely happy for a time. In this sense he has the least to lose from any possible scandal.

Gerald is in many ways the least to blame for the eventual fate of Eva. At the end of the play it is he who takes charge of matters. He also displays the calmest thinking about the identity of the Inspector, is the first to begin thinking about a way out for them all, and shows determination and courage in telephoning the infirmary to enquire about the possible presence of a dead girl. It is Gerald who suggests the possibility of there being more than one girl involved.

Gerald has a natural confidence and a commanding manner which makes that of Mr Birling seem rather forced and artificial. However, at the end of the play it is clear that he has not learned as much as Sheila or even Eric, and we might wonder whether his admitted involvement in the girl's eventual fate generated any real feelings of remorse. He says that he has admitted that he 'kept a girl' last summer, but expects Sheila still to accept the engagement ring at the end of the play. His assertion that all is now well puts him firmly alongside Mr and Mrs Birling in their hypocritical belief that everything can return to normal again, now that the Inspector and the dead girl have both been exposed as pretences. The final few lines of the play confirm for us how wrong and foolish this assumption is.

Inspector Goole

The Inspector is deliberately an enigmatic figure. We are told nothing whatsoever about him, apart from his name. All the Inspector ever says about his own situation is, 'I haven't much time.' He neither changes nor develops. Nothing about him is revealed that we did not already known at the beginning. In these respects, amongst others, he is very different to all the other characters in the play.

Inspector Goole's name is an obvious pun on 'ghoul', a malevolent spirit or ghost, a person interested in morbid or disgusting things. We might feel tempted to see him as some kind of spirit, sent on behalf of the dead girl to torment the consciences of the characters in the play. Or we might feel tempted instead to see him as some kind of cosmic policeman, a representative of Saint Peter, conducting some kind of inquiry as a preliminary to the Day of Judgement. We might instead simply see him as a forewarning of things to come, one of Ouspensky's 'chosen' people, as discussed in the section on Priestley's background on page 6. The truth is almost certainly that Priestley did not want to promote any single interpretation of who the Inspector 'really' is. The Inspector's dramatic power lies in the very fact that his real identity is mysterious, unresolved and somehow other-worldly. If his identity had eventually been revealed definitely as a hoaxer or as some kind of 'spirit', this would have spoilt the play's ending. It is the unresolved tension at the end of the play that is effective.

The stage directions say that the Inspector has to create 'an impression of massiveness, solidity and purposefulness'. We are also told that 'He speaks carefully, weightily, and has a disconcerting habit of looking hard at the person he addresses before actually speaking.' The Inspector is at all times careful to behave correctly, but there is a definite air of menace about his manner, which seriously intimidates the others.

Unlike all the other characters, the Inspector does not deviate from his moral position and is unwavering in the single-minded way he pursues his chosen line of investigation. He alone is certain of every one of his facts, although it is interesting to see how, after he leaves, every fact is seriously questioned by the other characters; but this is after he has left. Whilst the Inspector is actually present, nobody challenges his explanations of events.

Inspector Goole says his duty is to conduct an investigation, but the scope and range of his questions surprises the others, and he makes several judgements about character which they feel an Inspector would not normally make. He questions their claim to be respectable and honourable members of society, and he seriously undermines their complacent assumption that they are good and worthy people. All of them find this a shattering experience.

Those characters who resist telling him the truth suffer more than those who are more open. As the Inspector says after Gerald accuses him of becoming a little heavy-handed, 'Possibly. But if you're easy with me, I'm easy with you.' Notice, for example, how he makes no judgement upon Gerald, and deliberately tries to stop Sheila from blaming herself too much. However, he begins to lose patience with Mr Birling and bluntly tells him to shut up: 'Don't stammer and yammer at me again, man. I'm losing all patience with you people.' Mrs Birling resists the truth the most, and the Inspector is accordingly harshest with her: 'I think you did something terribly wrong....'

The Inspector persuades characters to reveal things about themselves which they would rather not, or have actually tried to conceal. Sheila is the one who points out that there is something about the Inspector which *makes* them tell him things. She says it is because he gives them a feeling that he already knows. This is reinforced by the way the Inspector challenges people, as when he insists that Mr Birling did know Eva Smith, or when he gets the truth out of Eric with a simple 'Well?'. The most dramatic example of the Inspector's ability to recognize untruth is when he directly, and successfully, accuses Mrs Birling of being an outright liar.

Priestley gives Inspector Goole several functions in the play. He acts as the story-teller, linking all the separate incidents together into one coherent life-story. He often supplies dates for events, or fills in background about the girl – the fact that she had no parents to go back to, for instance, no relatives, and no friends. He also behaves rather like a father-confessor to each character, helping them to see the extent of their involvement in the downfall of Eva Smith, and encouraging them to acknowledge their guilt, and repent. Significantly, the Inspector himself hands out neither forgiveness nor punishment. Each character is made to face up to the fact that they must find the courage to judge themselves, because only then will they have learned anything and be able to change themselves.

Sometimes the Inspector behaves as the voice of conscience, as when he says to Sheila and Gerald: 'You see, we have to share something. If there's nothing else, we'll have to share our guilt.' He gets people to admit to things which they have hidden, not only from others, but also sometimes even from themselves – painful things they have avoided facing up to. He points out that everyone has social responsibilities and that these become greater as people's privileges increase. Both Sheila and Eric acknowledge this with their observations that the Inspector 'inspected us all right' and 'was our police inspector all right'.

The Inspector also plays the traditional role of the policeman in the 'whodunnit' story, by slowly uncovering the truth through his commanding manner, careful questioning, piecing together of evidence and shrewd insight. The difference here, of course, is that whereas in a traditional 'whodunnit' mystery we would slowly have revealed to us the identity of the real criminal, in this play *everybody* is gradually revealed as a kind of accomplice to murder. Additionally, in a 'whodunnit' there would have been a terrible crime to solve, but it is one of the main points of *An Inspector Calls* that no one has actually done anything to Eva Smith which a court of law would describe as a crime.

We are left at the end of the play with the feeling that, although for the most part the Inspector's visit has been in vain, there is a possibility that Eric, and especially Sheila, may have learned enough to make them change their ways. Perhaps this will allow such people to begin changing the world into a more caring place. However, we can see from the reactions of Mr and Mrs Birling and, more worryingly, from those of Gerald, that the opposition to such change is very strong. The Inspector's threats of a lesson that 'will be taught . . . in fire and blood and anguish' may fall upon too many deaf ears to have enough impact. Audiences watching this play in 1945 or 1946 would presumably have felt only too acutely that the Inspector's prophecy had indeed come to pass in the years since 1912.

Eva Smith

Eva Smith is the only character whom we never meet. This is a very skilful dramatic achievement on Priestley's part, because she dominates the action almost from beginning to end, and we feel that we know her at least as well as any of the other characters, by the end of the play.

Through carefully placed snippets here and there we learn quite a lot about Eva: she was very pretty, had large dark eyes and soft brown hair. She was lively, intelligent, a good worker, warm-hearted, mature, and about the same age as Sheila, twenty-four.

Throughout the play, Eva is depicted as an innocent victim of the selfishness of others. She was a good worker, both at the Birlings' factory and in the shop, but she was sacked because of the indifference and spite of others. She was a grateful and affectionate girl for Gerald, but she was abandoned because she had become inconvenient for him. For Eric, she was a compliant outlet for his animal lust, his drunkenness and his loneliness, but she was made an accomplice to theft and the mother of what would have been an illegitimate child, because of his weakness. For Mrs Birling she was an outlet for her 'respectable' feelings of charity, but she was discarded as being not worthy of help when she did not fawn and pander enough to Mrs Birlings's feelings of self-importance.

Throughout each incident, we see how Eva is easy prey for the 'respectable' people in society. Even at the end, in her relationship with Eric, we see how in spite of the way she has been treated she retains an ability to show kindness, affection and finer feelings beyond the reach of all the other characters. When she meets Mrs Birling she refuses to play what would have been a devastatingly powerful card, that she would be the mother of Mrs Birling's grandson. She does not betray Eric, although this would almost certainly have guaranteed her better treatment. Whereas she had been the victim of exploitation by all the others, she refused to treat them in the same way, even though she was in a position to bring disgrace and scandal upon them. As Eva Smith sinks lower and lower, we see her as increasingly honourable and noble. This is the direct opposite of what we see in most of the other characters, except Sheila and to some extent Eric. This helps us to see the affinity between Eva and Sheila. We are left with the feeling that perhaps Sheila might have suffered the same fate as Eva, had it not been for luck and her essentially more privileged position in society.

The mystery of Eva Smith is a part of the larger mystery of the play, including the identity of the Inspector and the meaning of the final telephone call. Eva Smith and her fictitious counterpart, 'John Smith', represent the innocence of all people, who can sometimes be destroyed by the indifference of others, unless they accord them the dignity to which all human beings are entitled.

What happens in each act

Act One

Everyone except the Inspector is on stage at the start of the play, and in evening dress, whilst Edna, the maid, is clearing away the dinner plates and setting out the port, cigars and cigarettes.

A dinner party is in progress

Arthur Birling, a prosperous industrialist, is holding a celebration to mark the engagement of his daughter, Sheila, to Gerald Croft, who is the son of an even more prosperous business rival of Birling's, Sir George Croft.

Mr Birling compliments himself on the port, which he remarks is the same as that bought by Sir George Croft. Sheila Birling is still a little put out, because Gerald stayed away from her all the previous summer, although he says it was only because he was busy at the works. Sheila's brother, Eric, suddenly guffaws at this point, and amidst the embarrassment she accuses him of being 'squiffy' (slightly drunk), which he denies.

Mr Birling makes a toast to Sheila and Gerald. Sir George and Lady Croft are abroad and so cannot be present, but they have sent a cable. Mr Birling says he is not sorry that the celebrations are quiet ones, and that this night is the happiest of his life. He looks forward to the cooperation of his and Sir George Croft's companies.

Gerald gives the ring to Sheila

Amidst the toasts, Gerald produces an engagement ring which he gives to Sheila.

Mr Birling makes a speech in which he stresses his 'hard-headed' approach to life, and says that the world (apart from Russia) is in for a time of increasing prosperity. His speech is optimistic. He dismisses the possibility of war; and he praises the latest advances in technology, such as aeroplanes and the latest wonder in ships, the *Titanic*, which is due to sail 'next week'. He says that the future is bright and that the children of Sheila and Gerald will live in a world which will have forgotten class conflict and war scares. (This speech, incidentally, places the action of the drama precisely in time; the *Titanic* sailed on her maiden voyage from Southampton on Tuesday, 10th April, 1912.)

The ladies retire to the next room

As the ladies retire to the next room and leave the men to the port and cigars, as was the custom then, they take Eric with them, leaving Mr Birling alone with Gerald.

Birling hints at a knighthood

Mr Birling hints that he expects to get a knighthood in the next Honours List, and that this may ease the concern he thinks Gerald's mother has about Gerald marrying into a socially inferior family. Mr Birling jokes that all should be well for his knighthood, so long as his family behaves itself and does not get into the police courts.

Eric returns to join the other men, having left the ladies talking about clothes. Mr Birling points out how such things are tokens of self-respect to women. Eric lets slip 'I remember –', but catches himself before he says any more. Mr Birling, in an amused tone, says he expects Eric has been up to something, like many young people who have more money and time than he did when he was young. He makes another speech to the two men in which he stresses his basic values in life: that a man should look after himself, and his family if he has one, and take no notice of the 'cranks' who say that everybody should care for everybody else. He tells the other two that a man should mind his own business. At this moment the front door bell rings.

The doorbell rings – an Inspector has called
Edna enters to say that an Inspector has called, and that he needs to see Mr Birling about something important. Mr Birling is still a magistrate, and he and Gerald joke that the visit may be about a warrant, unless Eric has been up to something. Eric becomes uneasy and Mr Birling is becoming suspicious of him as Inspector Goole is shown in by Edna. Mr Birling does not recognize him, although he knows the local police quite well, and the Inspector agrees that he is new, having just been transferred. Inspector Goole has come, he says, about a young woman in the Infirmary who has swallowed disinfectant and thereby killed herself. The Inspector knows a lot about her, because she left a letter and a sort of diary which reveals that she used more than one name: her original name was Eva Smith, and she used to be employed in Mr Birling's factory.

Birling is shown a photograph
When the Inspector shows him a photograph he recognizes her, although the Inspector will not allow Gerald and Eric to see it.

Mr Birling recollects, with a prompt from the Inspector, that the girl left his factory about two years ago, at the end of September in 1910. He can see no connection between this and the girl's suicide, but the Inspector is not so sure.

We learn of Birling and the girl
Mr Birling recalls that the girl was one of the four or five ringleaders in an unsuccessful strike for more money; she was sacked after the strike failed. The Inspector annoys Birling by asking why he sacked her, and Eric sides with the girl, implying that her dismissal was harsh, although Gerald thinks that Birling was right. Birling says he has to keep costs down, and becomes annoyed with Eric and says he dislikes the critical tone which the Inspector is adopting. Birling points out that he plays golf regularly with the Inspector's Chief Constable, Colonel Roberts, although this seems not to bother the Inspector. He asks the Inspector whether the girl got into any kind of trouble after she left his works, or went on the streets. The Inspector's reply hints at secrets yet to be revealed.

Sheila returns – she learns of the girl's death
Sheila returns to find out why the men have not come through into the drawing-room, and discovers the Inspector. Mr Birling becomes cross when the Inspector stops her and tells her about the suicide, which she says has upset her, particularly as she has been so happy that night. Birling becomes less cross when the Inspector reveals that all three of them know something about the girl, and that he did not call to speak only to Mr Birling.

The Inspector explains that, after being sacked by Mr Birling, the girl was unemployed for two months, then she ran out of money, had no lodgings, no one to help her and had become half-starved. She was desperate; then she had a stroke of luck and got a job at Milwards, a well-known local fashion shop which Sheila goes to. This was at the start of December in 1910.

After a couple of enjoyable months she was told she would have to go, even though there was nothing wrong with the way she was doing her work; a customer had complained about her.

Sheila is shown a photograph
Sheila becomes agitated at this news, and when the Inspector shows her a photograph of the girl she runs from the room distressed. Mr Birling goes after her and to tell his wife what is going on.

What happens in each act

Eric would like to go to bed
The Inspector refuses to show Gerald the photograph and tells Eric, who says he would like to go to bed, that he had better not, because he may only have to get up again soon. Gerald thinks the Inspector is being rather heavy-handed and protests that they are respectable citizens, not criminals. The Inspector says that sometimes he cannot tell the difference between the two.

We learn of Sheila and the girl
Sheila returns and says that she has told her father that she was the customer who complained, and that she felt bad about the incident at the time and feels worse about it now. The Inspector says that she is only partly responsible for the girl's fate, like her father. When Eric asks what happened, Sheila explains that the girl, who was pretty, held a dress up against herself in the shop and it suited her. When Sheila tried the same dress on she caught sight of the girl smiling at the other assistant, Miss Francis, as if to say that Sheila looked awful in it. Sheila was rude to both of them and complained to the manager, saying that the pretty girl had been impertinent. She agrees that she was jealous of the girl and had never done anything like that before. She says that the staff at Milwards give her 'looks' sometimes, and that this must be why.

We learn of 'Daisy Renton'
The Inspector says that after this, the girls changed her name to Daisy Renton. At this, Gerald becomes agitated and gets himself another drink. As the Inspector leaves the room to find Mr Birling, Gerald admits to Sheila that he knew Daisy Renton, and she realizes that this is where he was all the previous summer. He says he has not seen her for six months. Gerald wants to keep this from the Inspector, but Sheila says that is impossible, because he *knows*. The door opens slowly. The Inspector returns, looks at them both searchingly and asks: 'Well?'.

Act Two

The Inspector begins to question Gerald
The Inspector looks at Gerald and repeats his question: 'Well?' Gerald sees that he is to be questioned, and tries to get Sheila to leave the room, but she will not go.

Gerald thinks that Sheila simply wants to see him 'put through it', as she was, but she says he is wrong. The Inspector explains that Sheila feels responsible for the girl's fate, and if she does not stay to hear Gerald's story, she will not see that it is only partly her fault. He says it is important for people to share their guilt.

Sheila sees something 'special' about the Inspector
Sheila realizes that there is something special about the Inspector.

Mrs Birling returns
Mrs Birling enters, full of confidence and quite out of key with the atmosphere so far. Sheila tries repeatedly to get her mother to drop the false social manner she is adopting, and to see that feeling pleased with herself will only make matters worse when the Inspector questions her. Mrs Birling takes no notice and continues in a very haughty way, accuses the Inspector of being impertinent, and reminds him that her husband was Lord Mayor and is still a magistrate.

Eric is exposed as a drunkard
The Inspector asks about Mr Birling and is told that he is looking after Eric. Mrs Birling says Eric has had a little too much to drink because of the celebrations, and becomes upset when Sheila points out that Eric has been drinking too much for the last two years. Gerald says he has gathered that Eric drinks 'pretty hard'. Mr Birling comes back without Eric, and the Inspector says he will see him later.

We learn of Gerald and the girl

The Inspector questions Gerald, who confesses that he knew Daisy Renton. He met her in a bar at the Palace Variety Theatre in Brumley, one where prostitutes were known to congregate, and rescued her from the advances of Alderman Joe Meggarty, whom he identifies as a notorious womanizer, drunkard and rogue, as both the Inspector and Sheila confirm, to the astonishment of Mr and Mrs Birling. Gerald and the girl went to the County Hotel for a drink and a talk. The girl told Gerald about herself: her name, that her parents were dead, that she came from somewhere just outside Brumley, that she had had a job in one of the works but had had to leave after a strike, and that she had had a job in a shop, although she was vague about this. Gerald was unable to get any exact details from her about her past life. She was broke and hungry, so Gerald made the hotel find her some food.

Gerald and the girl met again two nights later. Gerald's friend, Charlie Brunswick, had gone off to Canada for six months and left Gerald the use of his rooms in Morgan Terrace. Gerald insisted that the girl use the rooms, and gave her money to keep her going. Gerald explains to the Inspector that he did this without asking for anything in return, although he confesses that over a period of time they became lovers, although Gerald did not feel as much for her as she did for him. The suggestion is that neither of them really loved the other; she was grateful and affectionate, he was flattered. Sheila is very critical of Gerald, but recognizes his honesty. Gerald explains that the affair ended at the start of September, when he went away on business for a few weeks and the girl left the rooms, with a parting gift of money from him.

The Inspector says the girl's diary reveals that she went to a seaside place for about two months, and that she felt that she would never be as happy again – so she had to be quiet and remember, just to make it last longer. The Inspector allows Gerald, who says he is more upset than he may seem, to go for a walk.

Sheila returns the ring to Gerald; he goes for a walk

Sheila returns his engagement ring. She says that, although she now respects him more than she used to, they will have to start getting to know each other all over again, because they are both different people now. Gerald goes out.

Mrs Birling is shown a photograph

The Inspector shows a photograph of the girl to Mrs Birling, who says she does not recognize her. The Inspector accuses her of lying, and Birling becomes angry and demands an apology. Sheila realizes that her mother did recognize the girl in the photograph, and tells her parents to stop putting on a pretence, because they are making things worse. The front door slams and Birling goes to investigate.

The Inspector questions Mrs Birling about her part in the Brumley Women's Charity Organization. Under pressure, she admits that she was chairwoman of the committee which sat two weeks previously. Mr Birling returns to say that the door banging must have been Eric going out. The Inspector says he will have to be brought back soon, if he does not return, because he will be needed.

We learn of Mrs Birling and the girl

The Inspector resumes his questioning of Mrs Birling by saying that she saw Eva Smith at the committee meeting two weeks before, where the girl appealed for help. Mrs Birling admits this, and further admits that, because the girl called herself Mrs Birling, she was prejudiced against her case and regarded her as grossly impertinent. Mr Birling supports her in this. Mrs Birling says that the girl had only herself to blame for her fate, and that she lied about her circumstances: being married, husband deserting her, etc. The girl called herself Mrs Birling because she said it was the first name that came into her head, but the real Mrs Birling did not believe her, and says that her conscience is clear – the girl was not a good case, and Mrs Birling used her influence to have her application for help turned down.

We learn of the dead girl's pregnancy

The Inspector says that Mrs Birling is mistaken in her insistence that she has done nothing wrong, and reveals that the girl was pregnant. It was because of this that she went to Mrs Birling's committee for help. It is made clear to us that the father of the child is not Gerald Croft. Mrs Birling knew the girl was pregnant when she turned her down, and Sheila is horrified at this and calls her mother cruel and vile. Mr Birling thinks that this will go badly against them at the inquest. Mrs Birling points out that she was not the one who sacked the girl from her factory, and that the girl knew who the father was but was claiming 'elaborate fine feelings' and giving herself 'airs'. The girl said that the father was only a youngster who was 'silly and wild and drinking too much'. The father had given her money, but she felt that marriage would be wrong for both of them. Under further pressure from the Inspector, Mrs Birling admits that the girl said she did not want to take any more money from the father, because she suspected that he was stealing it.

Mrs Birling blames the baby's father
Mrs Birling blames the girl for her own circumstances and says that because she lied about being married, she may well have lied about other things, so Mrs Birling felt right to refuse her help. She places the blame also upon the father of the girl's baby, saying that this 'drunken young idler' should be made an example of, because the girl's death is due to him. Even if the story about his stealing money is true, it is still his responsibility, she says, because this was the reason the girl came to her committee. If he had not stolen the money, the girl would not have come to the committee, and would therefore not have been refused help.

Eric is exposed as the father
Sheila realizes that the father is Eric, and tries to quieten her mother, but Mrs Birling presses on, demanding that the Inspector make a public example of the father. Mr and Mrs Birling finally realize what the Inspector is driving at, and Mr Birling asks whether the Inspector is suggesting that the father is his son. The Inspector replies that Mrs Birling has made it quite clear what should be done if this is the case. The front door is heard, and Eric enters, looking pale and distressed. He looks at the others.

Act Three

Eric comes in
Eric knows that everybody else is aware of his part in things now. He is cross that Sheila has told the others about his drinking, but she says he is being unfair – she could have told on him months ago, and had only spoken up because it was obvious that everything was coming out. Mrs Birling is distressed and Mr Birling feels Sheila has been disloyal. The Inspector wants to hear Eric's side of things.

We learn of Eric and the girl
Eric says he met the girl in the Palace bar one night the previous November, when he got drunk. He went home with her, threatened to make a row unless she let him into her lodging, and made love to her, although he remembered none of it afterwards. Sheila and her mother leave the room at this point, on Mr Birling's instructions. Eric and the girl met several times after this, they made love again, and the girl became pregnant. Although they were both very worried about the pregnancy, the girl refused to marry Eric, because he did not love her. Eric gave her money to keep her going – about fifty pounds in all.

Eric is exposed as a thief
Mr Birling demands to know where Eric got the money from, and it emerges that he stole it from his father's office.

Sheila and her mother return
Mrs Birling and Sheila return at this point; Mrs Birling says she cannot stay out – she has to know what is happening.

Mr Birling tells his wife and daughter that Eric has admitted that he got the girl pregnant, and gave her money he had stolen from the office. Mrs Birling is shocked. Mr Birling is concerned to cover things up, but wants to know why Eric did not come to him for help. Eric says that Mr Birling is not the kind of father that a son could go to when he is in trouble.

The Inspector gets Eric to confirm that when the girl realized that the money was stolen, she would not take any more. Eric adds that she refused to see him again, although he wants to know how the Inspector knew about this. Sheila says that the girl told their mother. Eric is near breaking point and accuses his mother of being the murderer of the girl and her own grandchild. Mrs Birling says she did not understand. Eric says she does not understand anything, never did and never even tried. Sheila is frightened and Mr Birling is furious.

The Inspector makes a speech – then leaves
The Inspector intervenes to take charge again. He sums up by saying that there are millions and millions of Eva Smiths and John Smiths 'all intertwined with our lives' and that because people do not live alone, they are 'responsible for each other'. The Inspector threatens that if people cannot learn this lesson then they will soon be taught it 'in fire and blood and anguish'; and then he leaves.

Mr and Mrs Birling at once turn on Eric, blame him for everything, and say they are ashamed of him. Eric notes that all Mr Birling seems really bothered about is that he may not now get a knighthood. He says he is ashamed of them also. Sheila becomes angry at the way her parents seem to be ignoring the real lesson they should have learnt.

Was he really an Inspector?
Sheila comments that the Inspector arrived just after Mr Birling was telling Gerald and Eric that a man should make his own way, look after himself, mind his own business and ignore cranks who tell everybody to look after everybody else. Sheila wonder if he really *was* a police inspector. Mr Birling says that if he was not, then it changes everything, although Sheila disagrees. Eric agrees with Sheila. Birling accuses Eric and Sheila of letting the Inspector bluff them into telling him things he did not really know much about. As Mr and Mrs Birling are trying to think of a way out of what they now see as a malicious hoax, the door bell rings and Gerald returns.

Gerald returns
Gerald has come back from his walk, having met a police sergeant he knows, with the news that their caller was not a real police officer.

There is no 'Inspector Goole'
Birling telephones the Chief Constable, who confirms that there is no Inspector Goole in the police force. As far as Gerald and Mr and Mrs Birling are concerned, this changes everything, and they feel that all they have to do now is to keep calm and avoid a public scandal.

Eric, and especially Sheila, are horrified at the attitude of the others. They cannot understand how they can ignore the fact that this girl is dead, and that they all helped to kill her.

Was there more than one girl?
Gerald suggests that it may not even be just one girl – that perhaps there were several girls. He points out how the Inspector never showed the photograph to more than one person at once. He showed a photograph to Birling, and one to Sheila, but they may have been different photographs. Gerald was not shown a photograph at all, and had simply admitted to knowing a girl called Daisy Renton. They have only the Inspector's word that this girl was Eva Smith. Mrs Birling did not know the real name of the girl she saw at the Committee meeting, but was told by the Inspector that it was Eva Smith. The girl did not use that name to Mrs Birling. Again, the photograph she was shown by the Inspector was not seen by anybody else.

There is no suicide victim

Gerald and Mr Birling then wonder whether *any* girl had killed herself. Gerald telephones the Infirmary to check. The Infirmary say they have had no girl who has died there that day: no one had been admitted after drinking disinfectant, and they have not had a suicide for months. Mr and Mrs Birling are delighted, as is Gerald. They are convinced that it has been an elaborate hoax. Mr Birling tells Sheila that it is all over now, but she is unconvinced. Sheila cannot forget that all the things they confessed to really did happen. If there has been no tragedy then they have been lucky. Mr Birling treats the Inspector's visit as a joke, and makes fun of how Eric and Sheila took things so seriously. They are frightened by the way he talks. She is upset that they seemed to be starting to learn something, but now that has all stopped.

Gerald offers Sheila the ring again

Gerald thinks everything is all right now, and offers the ring back to Sheila. She refuses, saying that she must think about it.

The telephone rings – an Inspector is to call

Just as Mr Birling accuses Eric and Sheila of being unable to take a joke, the telephone rings. Birling answers it, then turns to the others, panic-stricken. It was the police. A girl has just died on her way to the Infirmary, having drunk some disinfectant. A police inspector is coming to call, to ask them some questions . . .

Coursework and preparing for the examination

If you wish to gain a certificate in English literature then there is no substitute for studying the text/s on which you are to be examined. If you cannot be bothered to do that, then neither this guide nor any other will be of use to you.

Here we give advice on studying the text, writing a good essay, producing coursework, and sitting the examination. However, if you meet problems you should ask your teacher for help.

Studying the text

No, not just read – study. You must read your text at least twice. Do not dismiss it if you find a first reading difficult or uninteresting. Approach the text with an open mind and you will often find a second reading more enjoyable. When you become a more experienced reader enjoyment usually follows from a close study of the text, when you begin to appreciate both what the author is saying and the skill with which it is said.

Having read the text, you must now study it. We restrict our remarks here to novels and plays, though much of what is said can also be applied to poetry.

1 You will know in full detail all the major incidents in your text, **why**, **where** and **when** they happen, **who** is involved, **what** leads up to them and what follows.

2 You must show that you have an **understanding of the story**, the **characters**, and the **main ideas** which the author is exploring.

3 In a play you must know what happens in each act, and more specifically the organization of the scene structure – how one follows from and builds upon another. Dialogue in both plays and novels is crucial. You must have a detailed knowledge of the major dialogues and soliloquies and the part they play in the development of plot, and the development and drawing of character.

4 When you write about a novel you will not normally be expected to quote or to refer to specific lines but references to incidents and characters must be given, and they must be accurate and specific.

5 In writing about a play you will be expected both to paraphrase dialogue and quote specific lines, always provided, of course, that they are actually contributing something to your essay!

To gain full marks in coursework and/or in an examination you will also be expected to show your own reaction to, and appreciation of, the text studied. The teacher or examiner always welcomes those essays which demonstrate the student's own thoughtful response to the text. Indeed, questions often specify such a requirement, so do parmicipyte iw those classroom discussions, the debates, class dramatizations of all or selected parts of your text, and the many other activities which enable a class to share and grow in their understanding and feeling for literature.

Making notes
A half-hearted reading of your text, or watching the 'film of the book' will not give you the necessary knowledge to meet the above demands.

As you study the text jot down sequences of events; quotations of note; which events precede and follow the part you are studying; the characters involved; what the part being studied contributes to the plot and your understanding of character and ideas.

Write single words, phrases and short sentences which can be quickly reviewed and which will help you to gain a clear picture of the incident being studied. Make your notes neat and orderly, with headings to indicate chapter, scene, page, incident, character, etc, so that you can quickly find the relevant notes or part of the text when revising.

Writing the essay

Good essays are like good books, in miniature; they are thought about, planned, logically structured, paragraphed, have a clearly defined pattern and development of thought, and are presented clearly – and with neat writing! All of this will be to no avail if the tools you use, i.e. words, and the skill with which you put them together to form your sentences and paragraphs are severely limited.

How good is your general and literary vocabulary? Do you understand and can you make appropriate use of such terms as 'soliloquy', 'character', 'plot', 'mood', 'dramatically effective', 'comedy', 'allusion', 'humour', 'imagery', 'irony', 'paradox', 'anti-climax', 'tragedy'? These are all words which examiners have commented on as being misunderstood by students.

Do you understand 'metaphor', 'simile', 'alliteration'? Can you say what their effect is on you, the reader, and how they enable the author to express himself more effectively than by the use of a different literary device? If you cannot, you are employing your time ineffectively by using them.

You are writing an English literature essay and your writing should be literate and appropriate. Slang, colloquialisms and careless use of words are not tolerated in such essays.

Essays for coursework

The exact number of essays you will have to produce and their length will vary; it depends upon the requirements of the examination board whose course you are following, and whether you will be judged solely on coursework or on a mixture of coursework and examination.

As a guide, however your course is structured, you will be required to provide a folder containing at least ten essays, and from that folder approximately five will be selected for moderation purposes. Of those essays, one will normally have been done in class-time under conditions similar to those of an examination. The essays must cover the complete range of course requirements and be the unaided work of the student. One board specifies that these pieces of continuous writing should be a minimum of 400 words long, and another, a minimum of 500 words long. Ensure that you know what is required for your course, and do not aim for the minimum amount – write a full essay then prune it down if necessary.

Do take care over the presentation of your final folder of coursework. There are many devices on the market which will enable you to bind your work neatly, and in such a way that you can easily insert new pieces. Include a 'Contents' page and a front and back cover to keep your work clean. Ring binders are unsuitable items to hand in for **final** assessment purposes as they are much too bulky.

What sort of coursework essays will you be set? All boards lay down criteria similar to the following for the range of student response to literature that the coursework must cover.

Work must demonstrate that the student:

1 shows an understanding not only of surface meaning but also of a deeper awareness of themes and attitudes;

2 recognizes and appreciates ways in which authors use language;

3 recognizes and appreciates ways in which writers achieve their effects, particularly in how the work is structured and in its characterization;

4 can write imaginatively in exploring and developing ideas so as to communicate a sensitive and informed personal response to what is read.

Much of what is said in the section **'Writing essays in an examination'** (below) is relevant here, but for coursework essays you have the advantage of plenty of time to prepare your work – so take advantage of it.

There is no substitute for arguing, discussing and talking about a question on a particular text or theme. Your teacher should give you plenty of opportunity for this in the classroom. Listening to what others say about a subject often opens up for you new ways to look at and respond to it. The same can be said for reading about a topic. Be careful not to copy down slavishly what others say and write. Jot down notes then go away and think about what you have heard, read and written. Make more notes of your own and then start to clarify your own thoughts, feelings and emotions on the subject about which you are writing. Most students make the mistake of doing their coursework essays in a rush – you have time so use it.

Take a great deal of care in planning your work. From all your notes, write a rough draft and then start the task of really perfecting it.

1 Look at your arrangement of paragraphs, is there a logical development of thought or argument? Do the paragraphs need rearranging in order? Does the first or last sentence of any paragraph need redrafting in order to provide a sensible link with the preceding or next paragraph?

2 Look at the pattern of sentences within each paragraph. Are your thoughts and ideas clearly developed and expressed? Have you used any quotations, paraphrases, or references to incidents to support your opinions and ideas? Are those references relevant and apt, or just 'padding'?

3 Look at the words you have used. Try to avoid repeating words in close proximity one to another. Are the words you have used to comment on the text being studied the most appropriate and effective, or just the first ones you thought of?

4 Check your spelling and punctuation.

5 Now write a final draft, the quality of which should reflect the above considerations.

Writing essays in an examination
Read the question. Identify the key words and phrases. Write them down, and as they are dealt with in your essay plan, tick them off.

Plan your essay. Spend about five minutes jotting down ideas; organize your thoughts and ideas into a logical and developing order – a structure is essential to the production of a good essay. Remember, brief, essential notes only!

Write your essay
How long should it be? There is no magic length. What you must do is answer the question set, fully and sensitively in the time allowed. You will probably have about forty minutes to answer an essay question, and within that time you should produce an essay between roughly 350 and 500 words in length. Very short answers will not do justice to the question, very long answers will probably contain much irrelevant information and waste time that should be spent on the next answer.

How much quotation? Use only that which is apt and contributes to the clarity and quality of your answer. No examiner will be impressed by 'padding'.

What will the examiners be looking for in an essay?
1 An answer to the question set, and not a prepared answer to another, albeit slightly similar question done in class.

2 A well-planned, logically structured and paragraphed essay with a beginning, middle and end.

3 Accurate references to plot, character, theme, as required by the question.

4 Appropriate, brief, and if needed, frequent quotation and references to support and demonstrate the comments that you are making in your essay.

5 Evidence that reading the text has prompted in you a personal response to it, as well as some judgment and appreciation of its literary merit.

How do you prepare to do this?

1 During your course you should write between three to five essays on each text.

2 Make good use of class discussion etc, as mentioned in a previous paragraph on page 75.

3 Try to see a live performance of a play. It may help to see a film of a play or book, though be aware that directors sometimes leave out episodes, change their order, or worse, add episodes that are not in the original – so be very careful. In the end, there is no substitute for **reading and studying** the text!

Try the following exercises without referring to any notes or text.

1 Pick a character from your text.

2 Make a list of his/her qualities – both positive and negative ones, or aspects that you cannot quite define. Jot down single words to describe each quality. If you do not know the word you want, use a thesaurus, but use it in conjunction with a dictionary and make sure you are fully aware of the meaning of each word you use.

3 Write a short sentence which identifies one or more places in the text where you think each quality is demonstrated.

4 Jot down any brief quotation, paraphrase of conversation or outline of an incident which shows that quality.

5 Organize the list. Identify groupings which contrast the positive and negative aspects of character.

6 Write a description of that character which makes full use of the material you have just prepared.

7 What do you think of the character you have just described? How has he/she reacted to and coped with the pressures of the other characters, incidents, and the setting of the story? Has he/she changed in any way? In no more than 100 words, including 'evidence' taken from the text, write a balanced assessment of the character, and draw some conclusions.

You should be able to do the above without notes, and without the text, unless you are to take an examination which allows the use of plain texts. In plain text examinations you are allowed to take in a copy of your text. It must be without notes, either your own or the publisher's. The intention is to enable you to consult a text in the examination so as to confirm memory of detail, thus enabling a candidate to quote and refer more accurately in order to illustrate his/her views that more effectively. Examiners will expect a high standard of accurate reference, quotation and comment in a plain text examination.

Sitting the examination

You will have typically between two and five essays to write and you will have roughly 40 minutes, on average, to write each essay.

On each book you have studied, you should have a choice of doing at least one out of two or three essay titles set.

1 **Before sitting the exam**, make sure you are completely clear in your mind that you know exactly how many questions you must answer, which sections of the paper you must tackle, and how many questions you may, or must, attempt on any one book or in any one section of the paper. If you are not sure, ask your teacher.

2 **Always read the instructions** given at the top of your examination paper. They are

there to help you. Take your time, and try to relax – panicking will not help.

3 **Be very clear about timing, and organizing your time.**

(a) Know how long the examination is.
(b) Know how many questions you must do.
(c) Divide (b) into (a) to work out how long you may spend on each question. (Bear in mind that some questions may attract more marks, and should therefore take proportionately more time.)
(d) Keep an eye on the time, and do not spend more than you have allowed for any one question.
(e) If you have spare time at the end you can come back to a question and do more work on it.
(f) Do not be afraid to jot down notes as an aid to memory, but do cross them out carefully after use – a single line will do!

4 **Do not rush the decision** as to which question you are going to answer on a particular text.

(a) Study each question carefully.
(b) Be absolutely sure what each one is asking for.
(c) Make your decision as to which you will answer.

5 **Having decided which question** you will attempt:

(a) jot down the key points of the actual question – use single words or short phrases;
(b) think about how you are going to arrange your answer. Five minutes here, with some notes jotted down will pay dividends later;
(c) write your essay, and keep an eye on the time!

6 **Adopt the same approach** for all questions. Do write answers for the maximum number of questions you are told to attempt. One left out will lose its proportion of the total marks. Remember also, you will never be awarded extra marks, over and above those already allocated, if you write an extra long essay on a particular question.

7 **Do not waste time** on the following:

(a) an extra question – you will get no marks for it;
(b) worrying about how much anyone else is writing, they can't help you!
(c) relaxing at the end with time to spare – you do not have any. Work up to the very moment the invigilator tells you to stop writing. Check and recheck your work, including spelling and punctuation. Every single mark you gain helps, and that last mark might tip the balance between success and failure – the line has to be drawn somewhere.

8 **Help the examiner.**

(a) Do not use red or green pen or pencil on your paper. Examiners usually annotate your script in red and green, and if you use the same colours it will cause unnecessary confusion.
(b) Leave some space between each answer or section of an answer. This could also help you if you remember something you wish to add to your answer when you are checking it.
(c) Number your answers as instructed. If it is question 3 you are doing, do not label it 'C'.
(d) Write neatly. It will help you to communicate effectively with the examiner who is trying to read your script.

Glossary of literary terms

Mere knowledge of the words in this list or other specialist words used when studying literature is not sufficient. You must know when to use a particular term, and be able to describe what it contributes to that part of the work which is being discussed.

For example, merely to label something as being a metaphor does not help an examiner or teacher to assess your response to the work being studied. You must go on to analyse what the literary device contributes to the work. Why did the author use a metaphor at all? Why not some other literary device? What extra sense of feeling or meaning does the metaphor convey to the reader? How effective is it in supporting the author's intention? What was the author's intention, as far as you can judge, in using that metaphor?

Whenever you use a particular literary term you must do so with a purpose and that purpose usually involves an explanation and expansion upon its use. Occasionally you will simply use a literary term 'in passing', as, for example, when you refer to the 'narrator' of a story as opposed to the 'author' – they are not always the same! So please be sure that you understand both the meaning and purpose of each literary term you employ.

This list includes only those words which we feel will assist in helping you to understand the major concepts in play and novel construction. It makes no attempt to be comprehensive. These are the concepts which examiners frequently comment upon as being inadequately grasped by many students. Your teacher will no doubt expand upon this list and introduce you to other literary devices and words within the context of the particular work/s you are studying – the most useful place to experience and explore them and their uses.

Plot This is the plan or story of a play or novel. Just as a body has a skeleton to hold it together, so the plot forms the 'bare bones' of the work of literature in play or novel form. It is however, much more than this. It is arranged in time, so one of the things which encourages us to continue reading is to see what happens next. It deals with causality, that is how one event or incident causes another. It has a sequence, so that in general, we move from the beginning through to the end.

Structure The arrangement and interrelationship of parts in a play or novel are obviously bound up with the plot. An examination of how the author has structured his work will lead us to consider the function of, say, the 43 letters which are such an important part of *Pride and Prejudice*. We would consider the arrangement of the time-sequence in *Wuthering Heights* with its 'flashbacks' and their association with the different narrators of the story. In a play we would look at the scene divisions and how different events are placed in a relationship so as to produce a particular effect; where soliloquies occur so as to inform the audience of a character's innermost emotions and feelings. Do be aware that great works of fiction are not just simply thrown together by their authors. We study a work in detail, admiring its parts and the intricacies of its structure. The reason for a work's greatness has to do with the genius of its author and the care of its construction. Ultimately, though, we do well to remember that it is the work as a whole that we have to judge, not just the parts which make up that whole.

Glossary of literary terms 79

Narrator A narrator tells or relates a story. In *Wuthering Heights* various characters take on the task of narrating the events of the story: Cathy, Heathcliff, etc, as well as being, at other times, central characters taking their part in the story. Sometimes the author will be there, as it were, in person, relating and explaining events. The method adopted in telling the story relates very closely to style and structure.

Style The manner in which something is expressed or performed, considered as separate from its intrinsic content or meaning. It might well be that a lyrical, almost poetical style will be used, for example concentrating on the beauties and contrasts of the natural world as a foil to the narration of the story and creating emotions in the reader which serve to heighten reactions to the events being played out on the page. It might be that the author uses a terse, almost staccato approach to the conveyance of his story. There is no simple route to grasping the variations of style which are to be found between different authors or indeed within one novel. The surest way to appreciate this difference is to read widely and thoughtfully and to analyse and appreciate the various strategies which an author uses to command our attention.

Character A person represented in a play or story. However, the word also refers to the combination of traits and qualities distinguishing the individual nature of a person or thing. Thus, a characteristic is one such distinguishing quality: in *Pride and Prejudice*, the pride and prejudices of various characters are central to the novel, and these characteristics which are associated with Mr Darcy, Elizabeth, and Lady Catherine in that novel, enable us to begin assessing how a character is reacting to the surrounding events and people. Equally, the lack of a particular trait or characteristic can also tell us much about a character.

Character development In *Pride and Prejudice*, the extent to which Darcy's pride, or Elizabeth's prejudice is altered, the recognition by those characters of such change, and the events of the novel which bring about the changes are central to any exploration of how a character develops, for better or worse.

Irony This is normally taken to be the humorous or mildly sarcastic use of words to imply the opposite of what they say. It also refers to situations and events and thus you will come across references such as prophetic, tragic, and dramatic irony.

Dramatic irony This occurs when the implications of a situation or speech are understood by the audience but not by all or some of the characters in the play or novel. We also class as ironic words spoken innocently but which a later event proves either to have been mistaken or to have prophesied that event. When we read in the play *Macbeth*:

> *Macbeth*
> Tonight we hold a solemn supper, sir,
> And I'll request your presence.
>
> *Banquo*
> Let your highness
> Command upon me, to the which my duties
> Are with a most indissoluble tie
> Forever knit.

we, as the audience, will shortly have revealed to us the irony of Macbeth's words. He does not expect Banquo to attend the supper as he plans to have Banquo murdered before the supper occurs. However, what Macbeth does not know is the prophetic irony of Banquo's response. His 'duties. . . a most indissoluble tie' will be fulfilled by his appearance at the supper as a ghost – something Macbeth certainly did not forsee or welcome, and which Banquo most certainly did not have in mind!

Tragedy This is usually applied to a play in which the main character, usually a person of importance and outstanding personal qualities, falls to disaster through the combination of personal failing and circumstances with which he cannot deal. Such tragic happenings may also be central to a novel. In *The Mayor of Casterbridge*, flaws in Henchard's character are partly responsible for his downfall and eventual death.

In Shakespeare's plays, *Macbeth* and *Othello*, the tragic heroes from which the two plays take their names, are both highly respected and honoured men who have proven their outstanding personal qualities. Macbeth, driven on by his ambition and that of his very determined wife, kills his king. It leads to civil war in his country, to his own eventual downfall and death, and to his wife's suicide. Othello, driven to an insane jealousy by the cunning of his lieutenant, Iago, murders his own innocent wife and commits suicide.

Satire Where topical issues, folly or evil are held up to scorn by means of ridicule and irony – the satire may be subtle or openly abusive.

In *Animal Farm*, George Orwell used the rebellion of the animals against their oppressive owner to satirize the excesses of the Russian revolution at the beginning of the 20th century. It would be a mistake, however, to see the satire as applicable only to that event. There is a much wider application of that satire to political and social happenings both before and since the Russian revolution and in all parts of the world.

Images An image is a mental representation or picture. One that constantly recurs in *Macbeth* is clothing, sometimes through double meanings of words: 'he seems rapt withal', 'Why do you dress me in borrowed robes?', 'look how our partner's rapt', 'Like our strange garments, cleave not to their mould', 'Whiles I stood rapt in the wonder of it', 'which would be worn now in their newest gloss', 'Was the hope drunk Wherein you dressed yourself?', 'Lest our old robes sit easier than our new.', 'like a giant's robe upon a dwarfish thief'. All these images serve to highlight and comment upon aspects of Macbeth's behaviour and character. In Act 5, Macbeth the loyal soldier who was so honoured by his king at the start of the play, struggles to regain some small shred of his self-respect. Three times he calls to Seyton for his armour, and finally moves toward his destiny with the words 'Blow wind, come wrack, At least we'll die with harness on our back' – his own armour, not the borrowed robes of a king he murdered.

Do remember that knowing a list of images is not sufficient. You must be able to interpret them and comment upon the contribution they make to the story being told.

Theme A unifying idea, image or motif, repeated or developed throughout a work.

In *Pride and Prejudice*, a major theme is marriage. During the course of the novel we are shown various views of and attitudes towards marriage. We actually witness the relationships of four different couples through their courtship, engagement and eventual marriage. Through those events and the examples presented to us in the novel of other already married couples, the author engages in a thorough exploration of the theme.

This list is necessarily short. There are whole books devoted to the explanation of literary terms. Some concepts, like style, need to be experienced and discussed in a group setting with plenty of examples in front of you. Others, such as dramatic irony, need keen observation from the student and a close knowledge of the text to appreciate their significance and existence. All such specialist terms are well worth knowing. But they should be used only if they enable you to more effectively express your knowledge and appreciation of the work being studied.